Routledge Revi

C000152360

Five Fast Per

First published in 1994, *Five Fast Pennies* was written by the Co-Founder of Food Lion, Inc., Ralph W. Ketner, to tell the story of the challenges and opportunities he faced throughout his life and career.

Accessibly written, the book provides a detailed insight into Ketner's philosophy of "Five fast pennies instead of one slow nickel", his views on success, and his journey from childhood through to Co-Founder of Food Lion, Inc. and beyond.

Five Fast Pennies

By Ralph W. Ketner

Routledge
Taylor & Francis Group

First published in 1994
Privately published

This edition first published in 2021 by Routledge
2 Park Square, Milton Park, Abingdon, Oxon, OX14 4RN
and by Routledge
711 Third Avenue, New York, NY 10017

Routledge is an imprint of the Taylor & Francis Group, an informa business

© Catawba College, 2020

Publisher's Note
The publisher has gone to great lengths to ensure the quality of this reprint but points out that some imperfections in the original copies may be apparent.

Disclaimer
The publisher has made every effort to trace copyright holders and welcomes correspondence from those they have been unable to contact.

A Library of Congress record exists under LCCN: 94220543

ISBN 13: 978-0-367-75675-8 (hbk)
ISBN 13: 978-1-003-16349-7 (ebk)
ISBN 13: 978-0-367-75672-7 (pbk)

Book DOI: 10.4324/9781003163497

Five Fast Pennies

by

Ralph W. Ketner

Co-founder, Food Lion, Inc.

Compiled by

Jason Lesley and Mark Wineka

Privately Published
Salisbury, North Carolina

Special Recognition to
Catawba College
and
Ralph W. Ketner School of Business
Salisbury, North Carolina

Printed in the United States of America
by
Salisbury Printing Company Inc.
Salisbury, North Carolina
1994

This book is dedicated to

Anne, my wife, who suggested and encouraged me to write
"Five Fast Pennies"

Linda, my daughter, and Robert, my son, for their
understanding of why it was necessary for me to spend
so very many hours working.

The millions of Food Lion customers who made possible
it's success.

The good Lord who gave me the ability, desire, and
opportunity to save Food Lion customers millions of dollars.

Table of Contents

Ralph W. Ketner

Forward

Why the title "Five Fast Pennies?"

I learned from my father, "Never charge the customer more than necessary. Make a living—not a killing." At **Food Town/ Food Lion,** our lower prices led to higher volume. We chose to make 1¢ profit on each of five cans of beans, instead of 5¢ on one can of beans—thus my philosophy of *Five fast pennies instead of one slow nickel.*

George Robert (Bob) Ketner
1888–1932

1. The Privilege of Being "Underprivileged"

They all thought I was going to die. Dad, my brothers and younger sisters, the doctor, too, I guess. There wasn't much way to fight pneumonia in 1926.

It had just killed my mother, and here I was 5 years old, burning up with fever, my lungs filling with fluid. The situation called for something drastic. The doctor decided to put a drainage tube in my side. There was one hitch: I was too weak for a pain killer. I remember they held my hands so the doctor could begin cutting and then — nothing.

It was winter when my mother and I got sick. I didn't know she had died for some time. I remember going outside for the first time and asking Grandma who put the leaves back on the trees.

I didn't realize it then, but I was 5 years old and my life was taking one of those turns that make a person who he is.

My dad, George Robert Ketner (everyone called him Bob) and my mother, Effie Yost Ketner, had married Jan. 11, 1911, and intended to raise a family on a farm near Rimertown. The Ketners were Pennsylvania Dutch farmers, migrants to North Carolina noted for thrift, ambition, hard work and a stubborn streak. Bob Ketner was no different.

He farmed and slaughtered animals and took the meat to Salisbury and sold it to the butcher shops. He saw the difference between what he was getting and what they were getting. And I believe it made him mad.

"I'm in the wrong end of this business," he told friends time and again.

In 1923, he moved the family—five children, soon to be six—to Salisbury and opened a little butcher shop at 501 N. Main St. While most stores were charging 35 cents a pound for pork chops, Dad charged 10 cents a pound. It wasn't long before he had a good business and added a full line of groceries.

He was a good merchandiser. He caught a shark on a trip to the ocean once and brought it back to put in the window. He had an "invisible" fish in an aquarium and once had a barrel labeled, "groundhog." Inside was a sausage: ground hog.

He operated a credit business at first. On the back of the ticket was printed: "You need your money, and I need mine. If we both get ours, that'll be fine. But if you get yours and keep mine too, what the hell am I going to do?" Eventually, he went to a cash and carry operation.

Dad believed that it was just as wrong to charge a price that was unfair as it was to shortchange a customer. His business mushroomed, and he had five stores in Salisbury and one in Kannapolis by the end of 1931. He kept prices low and increased volume, and I believe set the principles that led Food Lion to become America's fastest growing grocery chain into my head at an early age. If you give real value to your customers—save them money — they will reward you with their business.

Dad had a farm in Franklin where he raised 300 to 500 hogs and kept the farm at Rimertown. My Uncle Charlie ran the one in Franklin, and George Drye ran the one in Rimertown. I can remember driving down to visit the Dryes, and if they weren't at home, Dad would pull some trick on them. He was always pulling some trick on his friends. There was a fellow, Dave Bunyan, who always asked Dad to take him to a wheat threshing. He had heard about all the food they put out.

"Well, you've got to work if I take you down there," Dad told him. The man was willing to do anything, so Dad told him to bag the chaff. Ordinarily they just let it blow away. It's not worth anything. That poor man stood out there for 30 minutes in the summer heat about to die before Dad told him it was a joke.

Dad was heavy and muscular, but not fat. He must have weighed 220 pounds. He liked to bowl and sometimes drank white lightning made in the mountains. He'd pour a little into the cap of the jar and strike a match to it, looking for a certain color flame.

I loved it when he'd take me bowling with him. I was about 11 years old and he would bet on me against the men. Many times he would take me to the stores with him. I would have walked barefooted on fire to make him proud of me.

Sunday was our family day. Dad would come home from the farm and get a couple of big soup bones from the store and cook up some soup. He would send some in a cardboard oyster container to me at school for lunch. He didn't do much around the house, but he was pretty strict with his children. As long as you did what you were told, everything went along fine. But if I got a beating at school, I'd get another one when I got home. If we asked for money for firecrackers or something like that we'd seldom get it. Nonsense, Dad called it. At Christmas, we didn't get too many toys. But we got gold pieces or something of value, which really was a lot better than toys.

He really wanted the best for his children. I just didn't want what he was offering some of the time. We went to St. John's Lutheran Church with the upper class people of Salisbury, and when the time came for me to go to school, he enrolled me at Frank B. John, with the Country Club crowd, rather than at A. T. Allen, with the kids from my own neighborhood. I ran away from school every day and hid under the house. I lived on the rough side of the tracks, and I wanted to go to school there, too. When he put me at A. T. Allen, where everybody wore overalls and fought all the time, I got along fine.

I never considered myself a bad kid, just mischievous. Never drank or smoked. The biggest thrill in the world back then was go to bed without washing your feet. We'd go barefooted from May until October. We'd only wear shoes to church. Kids would make fun of you if you wore shoes during the week. I stepped on a thumbtack one day, and I thought I'd torn part of the skin on my foot. I hobbled around on the side of that foot all day, and it wasn't until I washed my foot that night that I found I had a thumbtack in it. I stepped on a rusty nail once and my foot got infected. The treatment was to tie a piece of fatback to it. Oh, we were rough compared to upper society in those days.

On Cemetery Street where we lived, there was not a blade of grass. Nobody ever thought about grass. You'd shoot marbles out in the front yard. It was level and dirt and you could sweep it clean. Kids would play under the house. Houses then sat up two or three feet off the ground. We would take a wooden box apart and cut out a toy gun. We'd cut out an inner tube and make a slingshot.

There was no TV. We didn't have money for the movies. We had to make our own entertainment. You fought all the time just to have something to do. I used to beat this one little boy to death. But one day the other kids convinced him that I was scared of him. Until then I could beat him. But when I came out that day, he socked the hell out of me because he had a mental attitude that I was scared of him.

Salisbury had a street car running up and down Main Street. Big fun was to call people on the phone and ask, "Is your house on the street car line?" And when they said yes, we'd say, "You better get it off. The car is coming." Or we'd call a store and ask if they had Prince Albert in a can. If they said yes, we'd yell, "Let him out!"

Life wasn't all play. Dad worked hard, and he expected us to work, too. I used to have to stay with my two younger sisters while Glenn, Ray, and Brown worked at the stores. They'd come home at 1 or 2 o'clock Sunday morning. The work started after they closed the store at 11 o'clock. They had to clean out the fish containers and haul everything out to the incinerator.

I'd be at home with my sisters with just a little coal grate to keep us warm. I'd keep a poker in there, and if anybody knocked on the door, I'd get that red-hot poker and we'd go to the door together. You didn't worry about anybody bothering you too much. I was scared of everything, graveyards especially.

After I got a little older, I was able to dress chickens. Bobby Harrison, who lived next door, and I would get a penny apiece to pluck the feathers off a chicken. Granddad, Luther Ketner, would chop their heads off, and they would flap all around the back yard. It was best to put a bushel basket over them until they quit kicking. If we broke the skin dressing one, it cost us a nickel. So we had to dress five free of charge to get even again.

The whole secret of plucking chickens is not getting the water too hot. If you leave them in there too long, you're just going to ruin everything. As soon as we'd get 20 cents, Bobby and I would head for the movies and a box of popcorn.

Granddad also cooked livermush in the back yard. He would cook pork off the bone and mix in cornmeal, and my older brothers' job was to stir that pot until it became solid. That was rough. My job was to split up logs with a wedge and a mallet.

Dad married Allene Glover, a clerk in one of his stores, in 1928. I'm not so sure she understood what a handful her step-children — me in particular — were going to be. There was one more big hitch. A real big one. Glenn was dating our stepmother's sister, Addie, and Dad didn't look too favorably on that. Addie took a job in Dayton, Ohio, and Glenn left home at age 16 to go to Dayton. He ran away, really, and for hours, they thought I had gone with him. I was playing in the guest bedroom and fell asleep under the bed.

Glenn got a job with Jewel Tea Company and within a few years became one of their top salesmen. He and Addie were married before they moved back home.

Even though I was just 10 years old, I was getting headstrong myself. If somebody said something that didn't suit me, I'd find a way to get what I wanted. Dad often bought live cows, and one of my favorite things was to get a bunch of boys and walk a cow the 16 miles to our farm at Rimertown. It would be an all-day lark and we'd take along something to eat and have a ball. Dad had a cow at the house in Salisbury, and I asked him if I could walk it to the farm.

"No I don't want it to go to the farm.," he said. "I am going to take it out to White Packing Company and get it killed."

He started to get in his car, and I said, "Where are you going?"

"Going to Spencer," he said.

I asked him if I could go along.

"I don't care what you do," he answered.

With that he drove off, and I told the kids, "Let's take the cow." They all reminded me that he had said not to take it to the farm. But I told them that the last thing he said was that he didn't care what I did. So we walked the cow to the farm. Generally, he would come to the farm and pick us up around 7 or 8 o'clock and bring us home, but finally about 2 o'clock in the morning, here came Dad in a truck. He told us the FBI and the sheriff were out looking for us. He knew where we were. The cow was gone.

My stepmother tried to make the best of our situation. Once she and Dad were going to the coast to fish with her brother and his wife, and she knew that I would have done anything to go along. She told me to hide in the back seat, and they wouldn't let Dad know I was in the car until we were 30 miles down the road, too far to backtrack and put me out. That was the only long trip I ever went on. I thought later that he knew all along I was back there.

I discovered right away that you couldn't do anything without money and I found all sorts of ways to earn it. The Capitol Theater held drawings for prizes during the Depression to get people to come to the movies. I would go to the show and stand in the lobby and ask people if they were going to be there for the drawing. If they weren't, they'd give me their ticket. I'd help the janitor sweep up, so he'd let me have all the tickets that had been thrown away. Every time they had a drawing, I would have 500, 600 chances. I won everything. People talked about how lucky I was. I wasn't lucky. I worked harder than anybody else. But the theater caught on and changed the rules so only adults could win. That killed that.

I made pocket money selling newspapers. The newsboys were great competitors and we'd do anything to beat each other out of a few pennies. One thing my pals and I learned early were tricks with the language. We would pull them on unsuspecting kids. For example, we would offer to bet on the score of a football game "before the game starts." That would always be 0-0, but there was always somebody naive enough to miss the trick.

Another bet that usually worked was to challenge some kid to say what two coins add up to 30 cents when one of them is not a nickel. It was surprising how many couldn't figure out the answer was a quarter and a nickel. Only one was not a nickel. But it was only a good idea to pull these tricks on somebody smaller than you.

I went to an auto race at the county fairgrounds one Sunday and noticed that nobody was selling food. I figured I would make a neat profit the next Sunday with some hamburgers. Unfortunately, about a dozen others had the same idea — and they went me one better. I hadn't thought about finding some way to keep my hamburgers hot; my competitors had. Cold burgers just didn't sell. I had to cut my price and lost half of my investment in the process.

One of my first real jobs was catching curb for DanDee Ice Cream. Before owner Dan Nicholas offered me the job he asked if I was afraid of any of the curb boys working for Honeydew, his competition next door.

"Let me go outside and look," I told him. I was no fool, even then. I looked 'em over and didn't think there was anything to worry about. People would pull their cars up to the curb on South Main Street and a boy from DanDee and one from Honeydew would jump on each running board. We had vanilla, chocolate, strawberry, pineapple, walnut, cherry, lemon, orange-pineapple, orange ice, butterscotch, honeymoon special, butterbrickle, Dan Dee Special, maplenut, popcorn and milkshakes, too.

I would say, "If you want ice cream talk to us, and if you want frozen water talk to them, because theirs isn't real ice cream." It paid a nickel an hour. From 1 p.m. to 11 p.m. on Sunday I made 50 cents. The word tip hadn't been invented. People nowadays would never let their children walk the streets in the middle of the night, but I certainly never thought anything about it. That's where the excitement was.

One Sunday night about 11:15, after 10 hours of working for Dan Nicholas, I was walking down the street and heard glass breaking. I thought something had happened at Dan's, but then I heard pistol shots. A city policeman checking the roofs of the buildings on Main Street found a sky light open at Belk's. He dropped through to check things out and two robbers took off through the front door — glass and all. The gunshots I heard were from the robbers and the policeman. Other policemen joined the chase and quickly captured the two and took them to the police headquarters, then located upstairs in the 100 block of West Fisher Street. I followed along and was there when the two were questioned.

They were told to put their hands up. They did so slowly and about halfway, but after being kicked in a certain spot, when again able, they followed instructions. When searched, they were found to have hacksaw blades taped inside their thighs to cut their way out of jail if there were arrested. They told the police they weren't trying to shoot them. The bullet holes in the windows were chest high. Everyone knew better. The two escaped from jail several days later.

I played the penny slot machines in Doc's Smoke Shop and vowed that if I was ever rich enough, I'd try the nickel machine. That would be something.

I had street smarts, but there was something about school that just brought out the worst in me. From first grade when I ran away from Frank B. John School until college, I always seemed to be on the wrong page: Like the first spanking I got in school. The teacher said, "The next one to talk will get a beating with a ruler."

I said, "I don't believe it will hurt."

The teacher said, "Come up here and I'll show you."

She slapped me on the hand. Boy, that hurts worse than on the rear end. In grammar school, I used to be in all the plays. I was to be George Washington in "Betsy Ross," and the part called for me to kiss some gal. That ended my performance. I was too embarrassed to do it. Ray "Swifty" Cauble said, "Let me have your part. I love kissing the girls." He could have it, brother.

It didn't take long to figure out that some of my teachers didn't like me. In fifth grade I had to write a theme on what I expected to be when I grew up. "I expect to be a man," I wrote. "When I get married, I expect to be a husband. When I have children, I expect to be a father." And I took it all the way down to great-great-grandfather. "When I die, I expect to be a corpse."

I got the biggest zero known to mankind. That's when I decided that I would concentrate on arithmetic because 48 times 42 is 2,016. I got a hundred. It didn't make any difference whether the teacher liked me or not. I always had a knack for arithmetic. If my brother Ray had a cashier out, he would send down to school and get me out of class to add grocery orders. The clerks wrote the prices down on the grocery bags, and then they'd take them to the machine and punch them in and add them. Even in grammar school, I could add faster than a machine.

Things seemed to be going pretty well for the family over the next few years. Brown made life hard for me, but what is an older brother supposed to do? I was often the guinea pig. I was playing baseball in a field and jammed a weed into my leg. Brown got his biology tools and operated on my leg. Another time, Brown saw a knife-throwing act in the movies and got Bobby Harrison and me to stand in front of the garage door so he could throw ice picks at us. We were lucky to live.

We never wanted to tangle with Brown. He was rough. But he is my favorite brother. He sued me later, but he's still my favorite brother. He's the only one who ever lent me any money. Ray was a ladies' man, the good-looking one. Brown was the character, the comedian. Glenn was the smart one, the only one who ever had a nickel. He's the sharpest man I've ever known. I'm no fool, but he's sharper than I am. My sisters, Dorothy and Virginia, were easier to get along with than my brothers. Dorothy married a Lutheran minister, Stafford Swing. Virginia was sharp as a tack. She went to college at 15. She married David Petty, past president of the North Carolina Gideon Association.

We are a stubborn bunch, often in disagreement. But I feel close to every one of them. Brown wrote this poem about his brothers and sisters:

The Ketner Clan

As different as night and day,
As alike as peas in a pod,
each insists on having his own say,
Even when talking to God.

They are never more together
than when they are apart;
never more apart
than when they are together.

Vociferous and argumentative
best describes their style
when discussing any topic,
no matter how far-out or mild.

You think you've backed 'em in a corner;
That they'll have to surrender — admit you're right!
Then you hear that scornful phrase,
"Surrender Hell; I've just begun to fight!"

There's a quaint quality about them,
I'm sure you will agree,
The smartest ones among them
always agree — with me!

When you see them in Heaven,
approach with utmost care
lest you disrupt their argument
and they find they're not alone up there.

by: C. Brown Ketner

Crazy things always seemed to happen to Brown. He was lifting a barrel of salted hides once and cut his finger and got lockjaw. He couldn't eat, and they had to knock one of his teeth out so they could get a straw through to give him liquids. The doctors told Dad that they had a shot that sometimes worked and sometimes didn't. It could cure him or kill him. Dad told them that they didn't have much choice. Thank God, the shot worked.

I wish that Dad had been as lucky. He got sick with stomach pains in 1932 and his doctor was out of town. Another doctor diagnosed his problem as constipation, but the real problem was an infected appendix. It burst. He died at age 43. A psychologist once told me that my father's death caused me to block out certain things, that I decided to let nothing get to me. He said I had an inferiority complex. That's why I always had to be the best. In any event, we were never the same.

His death sent our family off in different directions. I like to think that Ketner's Cash and Carry would have been like Winn-Dixie if Dad had lived. Four boys. We had the farm. We would have kept opening stores and growing. There was really no limit to what we could have done together.

But it all ended in 1932. Dad had no will, and each of the stores was sold. Ray bought one. Glenn took the one in Kannapolis. The others were sold. There was money, but my world sure seemed to be crashing down on me. Brown and Ray both moved out. My stepmother told me we were moving to Deland, Fla.

I couldn't find a part-time job in Florida and for the first time had to ask my stepmother for spending money. I was miserable. I stayed down there from September until December, and I told Stepmother I was leaving. I was going to ask Grandma to let me live with her. I found out later that my stepmother and Glenn had decided I should go to Oak Ridge Military School. I got the catalog, not knowing it was a discipline thing. Boy, I couldn't wait. I was telling them how much I appreciated it, and it would be wonderful. When they found out that I wanted to go, they wouldn't let me.

We moved back to North Carolina, and I went back to Boyden High School in Salisbury right after Christmas. It didn't take long for things to get stirred up. I went into Ms. Cossie Rice's room for English. She looked up and saw me.

"You're not in my room." she said.

"Yes ma'am, I am."

"You're not in my room," she said again.

She had no reason to pick on me. But she recognized me as a Ketner. "You're not going to be in my class," she said a third time. With that, the bell rang. "I must have the wrong room," I said.

She breathed a sigh of relief. She had had all the Ketners she intended to have.

I loved a good time, but good times cost money and I had to work, too. I could work for hours, then play for hours and get by with just a little sleep. Often, I would hitchhike to Kannapolis, about 15 miles south of Salisbury, and work at my brother Glenn's store from 5 a.m. Saturday until 2 a.m. Sunday.

Glenn had one rule: Nobody could work more than 24 hours a day. I'm not knocking him. He worked long hours too. But he had no sympathy for anybody who didn't enjoy working.

Those were the days when the clerk got the items the customer wanted. There were no shopping carts or self-service. If a customer wanted a box of matches, you walked to get it. You got back, and he wanted a box of soda. It was right beside the box of matches a hundred feet away, and you walked to get it. The cash register had six drawers, one for each clerk. At the end of the day Glenn would know who had produced the most sales. I would work right through lunch and dinner so my sales would be the highest for the day. I always tried to be the best and generally was.

I remember once I had an ingrown toenail and I split it with a razor blade so I could keep working. Boy, your tail is dragging after 21 hours of steady walking. Every day was rough, but when we finished work on Sunday morning, I would get with my brother, Ray, who also worked for Glenn, and the Monroe brothers, and we would drive 180 miles to Myrtle Beach, S.C. At the beach we would hide behind some bushes and change into swim trunks. About sundown Ray and his friend, Phil Monroe, would drive down to Pawley's Island to date girls who lived there. Phil's brother, Jim, and I would hang around the pool room or bowling alley until our brothers picked us up around 2 o'clock Monday morning. They would drive the rest of the night. We'd get home by 6 a.m.

In four years of high school, I don't think I ever took a book home. Stepmother was always extremely nice to me — though she wouldn't let me drive her car. But I pretty much had free rein. A couple of times I got expelled, and I paid my sisters a dollar or two not to tell on me. It was never for anything bad. Like one day John Willett said to me, "Let's ask Mr. Nettles, dean of boys, if we can take off and go to the ball game?" We asked and he said, "No," just like I thought he would, but that didn't stop John.

"We gave him a chance," John said, "now let's go anyway." We got up to about Fulton Street and a car pulled up. It was John Nettles, and he asked us if we were going somewhere. "Yeah," I said, "back to school." He expelled us both for a few days.

That didn't stop me from attending ball games on Fridays, but I did try to be careful and sign up for "crip" courses — the kind that required no homework or thought outside the classroom. I especially looked for a teacher who didn't care whether I attended every class. French was one of my mistakes. I was in Miss Emma Marston's class and she asked me in front of the entire class on a Monday if I had cut her class on Friday to go to a game. I admitted that I had.

"Well, I just want you to know that if you do that again, no matter what your grade is in this course, you'll fail it," she said.

"I think you mean that, Miss Marston," I said. "And since I'm positive I'll miss this class again, it would be foolish for me to waste any more time in here." So I got up and left. That's just like in business. When you see that somebody isn't going to work out, go ahead and let him go. It's best for everybody.

I did have some moments of glory in high school. The sophomore class took the Scholastic Achievement Test, and I made the highest grade in the class. But when the awards were presented there were only freshman, junior and senior. I didn't think anything about it. But my homeroom teacher said, "Ralph, I'm proud of you. You made the highest score in the sophomore class." They didn't want anybody to know I made the high score. They didn't publicize that at all. I never claimed to be the smartest one in the class. Most people don't know how to take a test. They tell you if you don't know an answer to skip it and come back later. But most people aren't smart enough to put an X out to the side to know where to come back to. I was smart enough to do that. So I could get back to mine more quickly than they could. Many were smarter than I, but they weren't smart enough to know that. The arithmetic was the reason I had the high score. Dad was good in arithmetic. It runs in the family. We've had arguments as to who was the best. But I'm the best. Ain't no two ways about it.

In business arithmetic, the teacher put a column of figures on the board and said, "This is how to add it."

"That's not the best way," I said.

She asked me if I could do it better.

"Yes, Ma'am," I said, "much better."

"Well come up and show the class," she said.

I got up there and added a few strings of figures in a matter of seconds, and she said, "OK, Ralph can add any way he wants. The rest of you have to do it this way." Then she started putting up problems like, "What's the interest on $185 for nine days?" Well, you know what that is. That's 27 3/4 cents. So I'd shout out the answer and everyone would write it down, knowing it was right. Finally one day she called me up.

"Ralph, if you promise not to come back in my room," she said, "I promise to give you a straight A."

And I never went back.

I was looking for another crip course when I signed up for geometry. I had made A's in business arithmetic, algebra and advanced algebra. But this was something entirely different. Near the end of the course I had a 25 average. Clifford Beck, the teacher, said, "Ralph, I don't want you to get your hopes up. You won't be able to graduate. You failed geometry."

"Mr. Beck," I said, "have you thought how it's going to look on your record if I fail under you? Last year, I had Miss Groves, the principal and your boss, for advanced algebra and had a 98 average. Now you fail me. If I fail, she's going to wonder about your teaching ability. This is the first year you've ever taught. You owe it to yourself to pass me so it doesn't become an issue.

"Let me think about it," he said.

And the next day he called me in and said I had a C-minus, the lowest grade I could get and still get out. He was a smart cookie. That same Mr. Beck later earned his Ph.D. in physics and joined the research team at the Oak Ridge Atomic Energy facility in Tennessee during World War II and made significant contributions to the development of the atomic bomb.

Thanks to Mr. Beck, I graduated from Boyden High School and started on the next chapter of my life. It was to be at Tri-State College in Angola, Indiana. Why Tri-State? It was the college farthest away from home that sent me a catalogue. I wanted to get away from home and away from Salisbury.

Tri-State College in Angola, Ind., seemed perfect for me for two reasons: (1) It didn't have dormitories. You lived in private homes, and I was a wallflower. I just didn't mess around at all, didn't date or anything. I had so many pimples on my face, I later had trouble shaving.

And (2) you started on your major the day you arrived.

Something else unique about Tri-State was that it started a new curriculum every three months, so students could drop out and work for three months, then come back.

My brother, Glenn, drove me up there to enroll in September 1937 and the first Sunday after I got settled we went to Sunday school. Now I was soon to turn 17, and I couldn't read anything in public. Wouldn't even say my name in front of a class, and they called on Mr. Ketner to read out of the Bible. I looked around, thinking there must be another Mr. Ketner in the class, but they were talking about the young Mr. Ketner. The passage had words like Nebuchadnezzar. I was too embarrassed to read it. I turned red. It's a wonder the church didn't burn down. That's the last time I ever walked in that church. I did attend other churches.

For my living arrangements, I got a room in a professor's home with two or three others. One was Gilbert Gable from Dayton, Ohio. He was in business administration. (Tri-State was considered one of the top engineering schools in the country.) A lot of the college boys were older and made fun of the way I talked. They'd ask me to say "oil" and then laugh at my Southern accent. I felt like a fish out of water. I had grown up with no social graces and on the wrong side of the tracks. I just couldn't feel at ease with high-falutin' people. I didn't mind talking to anybody one-on-one. As long as you didn't put me in front of the class, I'd argue with anybody.

I had an extremely good average in accounting. I had Professor Herring. On the first day of school he asked how many people had had bookkeeping in high school. About half the hands in the class went up, and I thought "Oh boy, now I've had it. I'm at a disadvantage." Then he said, "You're the ones I feel sorry for. If you've had bookkeeping you already know what I'm going to start teaching, and you're not going to pay attention. But

19

you're going to wake up one day and we will have passed you. And you'll never catch up again."

On the first day of English class, the professor, Mrs. Parrot, wanted each of us to stand and spell a word. She called on me to spell assignee but pronounced it "ASS-n-ee." I couldn't spell it. I hadn't even heard of it. The next person spelled it as-SIGN-ee, and I told her that anybody could spell assignee. She had mispronounced it. I guess I had to get mad before I'd speak up in class. She stood by her pronunciation, and the dictionary agreed with her.

I was in an industrial management course and our professor got up one day and said 64 times 12 1/2 is 798. I told the guy next to me that 800 was the right answer. I didn't correct the professor in front of the whole class. I wasn't that stupid, but the guy shot up and said "Ketner says you're wrong." The professor was using a slide rule, an instrument I had never seen. He didn't acknowledge the mistake right away, but as he made more multiplication errors, I would tell my friend. He would shoot his mouth off. As the class came to an end, the professor asked me to stay. He said his slide rule was slightly off and wanted to know what kind I had been using. I said I'd never heard of a slide rule. I was doing the calculations in my head. I'm not sure he believed me.

I started paling around with some high school students at the pool room and the bowling alley. One of them asked if I'd like to come and live at his house. His family had a little grocery store, and his mother let me eat with them. Before I left Salisbury I had gotten my learner's permit to drive. It was only good for 30 days, but I would erase the date when it expired and make it good for 30 more days. My friend had a Model A Ford, the first car I ever drove in my life.

I got through that first year and came home for the summer. I went down to Holshouser's Esso station on the corner of Monroe and Main streets where Jake Littleton, a friend of mine, was working at night, trying to make a few dollars. I convinced Jake to come to college and work his way through. He said he didn't have any money. I said maybe his sisters would send him 50 cents a week. "Your dad works on the railroad and you can get up there for free," I told him. To cap it all off I told him I'd find him a job. I didn't have one, but I told him I could get him one. The funny thing is that Jake graduated, and I didn't. He became president of two companies. I introduced him to his wife. I feel good about that.

Jake and I lived in the Kling boarding house in Angola. They had a son, Bobby, 12, who was taking boxing lessons. Bobby was aggravating us one night, so I held him while Jake put pea-nut butter in his hair. Needless to say, we were on his "list" for some time. He later became a Golden Gloves champion as well as the Navy champion. He was good. Years later, he looked me up at the Food Town office on Julian Road and said he had come to beat the hell out of me. I must have looked dumbfounded. It took a few minutes before I recognized Bobby Kling and was sure that he was joking.

The first year I was at Tri-State, I decided to join three other students in moving to a lake cottage three miles from school. None of us had a car — very few did in 1937. We made this de-cision in late September when the weather was great. My three buddies moved to the cottage in October, but I couldn't, as I hadn't received money from home. The snow arrived before my money did. One day of walking three miles each way in the snow ended their enthusiasm. They moved back to town the next day.

Angola, Indiana, was a small town with one bowling alley and a pool room. It was 50 miles north of Fort Wayne. There wasn't much to do there. A bunch of fellows planned to go up to Canada across from Detroit and asked if I wanted to go along just to help pay expenses. Now this is how naive I was. I was afraid to go because I didn't speak French so I couldn't order what I wanted to eat. I could think up hundreds of things to be afraid of in those days.

I enjoyed my accounting courses and business law, even though I'd cut business law if I thought the professor was going to call on me to read the lesson in class. By the summer of 1939 I had run out of money as well as ambition. I might have graduated if it hadn't been for public speaking. I dropped out of the course five times when it was my turn to make a speech. I just couldn't bring myself to do it. Years later — when I was back in Salisbury in a Toastmasters course — I heard Raymond Ritchie stand and give a talk on his business, Cheerwine Bottling Co., and I thought that I would be the happiest person on earth if I could do that. The person conducting the course criticized him pretty heavily for errors he had made and for running out of the room when he finished. But he ended the critique by saying that at least he hadn't fainted this time. That got me to thinking that all the worry and fear of looking foolish was just something I was imagining. I started to get a grip on my biggest fear.

In 1982, Tri-State asked me to be commencement speaker. I said I didn't qualify. A commencement speaker should be one of three things: a politician, a preacher or a graduate of the college. The president explained that every other year they wanted a graduate. Reluctantly, I agreed. Later they called wanting my topic, and I told them "Four-Letter Words, The Keys To Success: Home Work, Hard Work, Team Work, Good Luck, Good Lord, and a Good Idea." They gave me an honorary degree, and my family gave me the high sign from the audience that I hadn't embarrassed them too badly. And then they announced that the board of trustees had decided that my 43 years of business experience exceeded the six months I needed to graduate, and they made me a member of the Class of 1982 with a B.S. degree in business administration.

"You've ruined my talk," I told the president of the college. "I tell everybody that I didn't finish college. Now I've got to tell them that I did."

"Well," he said. "Tell them it took you 43 years to do six months work."

2. Cannon Mills

I left Tri-State College and came back to work for my brother, Glenn, at his store in Kannapolis. I could use my ability with numbers to add customers' orders, but my new-found accounting skills were of little value.

My buddy Joe Ridenhour left Glenn's store to go to work for Cannon Mills. He had connections there. Son of a Methodist minister, he couldn't afford to go to college, but Gray Bost, treasurer at Cannon Mills, had paid his way to Duke University. It wasn't a surprise when Joe left the grocery store for a job at Cannon. It wasn't long before Joe asked if I would like to work there too. He made me an appointment for a job interview.

The day of the interview was like speech class all over again. I walked around the big lake in front of the plant about five times before I got up the courage to go inside and sign the reception book. I went up to see Mr. Bost and Steve Miller, the head of accounts payable. I was so nervous I was stuttering. A few minutes seemed like an hour.

They asked me about my handwriting, and I thought they had seen the register where I'd signed my name. I said I was a little nervous and that I could write better than that.

They asked how I was in arithmetic.

"Damn good," I said.

They laughed and said they'd finally found something I didn't mind saying. They gave me a job in accounts payable making 37 1/2 cents an hour — $15 a week.

I worked two weeks and decided I was going to quit. It was a big office with a big clock on one wall. Fifty people would sit down at 8 o'clock, and they had better not leave their desk, except to get a file, until 12 when a little bell would ring. There was no such thing as a coffee break. One morning I was determined that I wouldn't look at the clock until the bell rang. It would be a test of willpower.

I worked for what seemed like 10 hours. The bell hadn't rung. And worked another 10 or 20 hours. The bell still hadn't gone off. I couldn't resist it any longer. It had to be one minute till 12. I looked up and it was 10 o'clock. That did it. I marched straight into the boss's office and told him that I had just worked 40 hours and got paid for two. "What do you mean? he said."

"I'm just not going to work at a job I hate this much," I said. "Any fool can do what I'm doing."

"Well, would you like to have my job," he asked, sarcastically.

"I don't want anybody's job," I said. "I'm just going to quit."

"Will you try it two more weeks?" he asked.

"I won't try it two more minutes," I said.

"If I put you on something else, will you try it?" he asked.

"You put me on something that requires a little intelligence, yes, I'll try it," I said. "I won't guarantee that I'll stay, but I will try it."

Things improved after that, and they turned around completely when I went to the vault one day and saw an invoice that said 2%, 10 days and noticed that the company hadn't taken the discount for prompt payment. I pulled three years of ledger cards without anybody knowing it and found they hadn't taken a discount in three years.

"Write this letter to Buffalo Chemical and you'll get a $3,300 discount," I told the boss. Cannon bought chemicals by the freight car. He got back five years of my salary with one letter.

And there were other things. They were buying something at 19 cents each. They got 12 1/2 percent discount. Well, that's 1/8, and 1/8 of 19 cents is 2 3/8 cents. They were dropping the 3/8 because it was less than a half. That's all right on one. You only lose 3/8 of a cent, but if you buy 10,000, that's $37.50. I researched all that and got the money back. It's a wonder Cannon Mills survived. I even wondered if somebody was being paid not to take those discounts.

Every couple of months I would tell Joe Ridenhour that I was thinking about quitting. He would talk with the treasurer about getting me a raise. I must have gotten six raises the first year I was there. One day, I told him that I thought it was time for another raise.

"I know what you've been doing," he said. "You've been using me to get you a raise. You're just not worth another raise."

I thought for a minute and told him that I would have to quit.

"What do you mean?" he asked.

"I can't work for a company that overpays me," I said. "It's against my principals."

"I don't think you're overpaid," he said.

"Joe, you just said they're not underpaying me," I said. "Now you're saying they're not overpaying me. So you're saying that out of all the money in the world, they've chosen the right payment to pay me? Mathematically, that can't happen. Either I'm overpaid or underpaid, one way or the other."

Joe just shook his head and walked away.

Even with the raises, I was always strapped for money. My brother Brown would lend me a few dollars if I needed it, but one weekend I was nearly broke and a girl invited me to go to Lenoir-Rhyne College for a football game. We weren't really dating, but there were three couples in one car and on the way back, they decided to stop for hamburgers. I'd spent every penny I had, so I played like I was sick and couldn't get out of the car.

Another time, I had two passes to get in the gate at the Metrolina Fair in Charlotte and offered one to a buddy with a car. He had little money for gas, so I ended up giving my other pass to a person buying the gas. Now, I had no pass. Another friend wanted to go, so the four of us headed for Charlotte. Near the fairgrounds, the two without passes got into the trunk of the car thinking we would get in for free. No such luck. The parking area was outside the gate.

I was still a wallflower in those days, but occasionally I could manage the courage to ask a girl out. One of the worst things I ever did was take a girl to the ballpark in Kannapolis. There wasn't a game scheduled that night. She asked what we were going to do, and I told her that one of my friends had bet me I couldn't get to first base with her. I struck out.

In January 1942, I felt certain I was going to get a raise because of my performance. That month it was announced that everyone working for Cannon would get a five percent increase in pay. This increase was to allow Cannon to stay competitive with salaries paid in defense plants. When I received my check for January, I got the five percent increase received by everyone but not the merit increase I expected.

The day after I received my January check, I went to Mr. Willer's office and asked about my raise.

"I've seen everything in my life," the boss said. "I thought you'd never surprise me, but I've never seen a man get a raise on Friday and ask for another one on Monday."

"Oh, did I get a raise Friday?" I said. "I apologize, I just didn't mean this. How much was it?"

He said it was 5 percent.

"You're not talking about the 5 percent increase?" I asked.

Yeah, he said.

"That's not a raise," I said. "Everybody got that. I've worked my tail off and was entitled to a raise. Now because everybody gets 5 percent, you're counting that as my raise? I quit."

I didn't win that battle.

Back when I went to work at Cannon Mills, I moved into Mary Ella Hall, a big rambling dormitory next to the YMCA in Kannapolis. Room and board was $5 a week. Cannon had a rule. If you got kicked out of the dormitory, you got fired. I kept telling the boss that someday I was going to get kicked out of Mary Ella Hall because the food was terrible. You've heard of chipped beef on toast? They tried to make it with bacon without first frying the bacon. I sent post cards to friends addressed to "Ptomaine Tavern." The mailman delivered it to Mary Ella Hall.

Mr. Sharpe ran it, and he seldom did business with people who didn't make donations to the baseball team. He bought good food but paid more wholesale than Glenn charged retail. I knew because I approved his invoices. I made a list of overpayments and showed it to my boss. It wasn't long before the head man at Mary Ella Hall called me in.

"I understand that you don't like it here too well," he said.

"I love it here except for the food," I said. "It could be better."

"Maybe you ought to move," he said,

"It's not that bad," I said.

"Well, let's change it," he said. "You've got to move."

"You're telling me, I'm kicked out?" I asked.

"That's right," he said. "I'm telling you that you are kicked out."

I went to my boss, Mr. Miller, and told him the news. He said that I'd lose my job, and I told him there were no hard feelings. He told me to wait around until he had talked with Mr. Bost, Cannon treasurer.

He came back with a smile on his face. "We're not firing you," he said. "But for God's sake, Ralph, wherever you go when you move out, calm down a little bit."

I had saved them thousands of dollars making 15 bucks a week. They made an exception for me on that.

I had no idea that things were only starting to get wild. I moved into a boarding house and roomed with Alan Hayes, brother of Bob Hayes, mill owner Charlie Cannon's son-in-law. I thought we were getting along just fine when one night I came in from taking a shower at the end of the hall and saw an envelope on the floor. I picked it up and put in on his dresser. "Whose dresser is that anyway, mine or yours?" he asked.

"What's the matter with you?" I asked.

And he got out of bed and asked if I wanted to make something of it. I said yes, and he knocked the hell out of me.

I had a big cut over my eye and a big cut on my lip. I didn't even know we were fighting. "Wait a minute," I said. "Stop this thing a little bit. Let me go in and stop the bleeding. We'll start over, and both of us will play for keeps."

I finally got the bleeding stopped, but it was pretty obvious that if he touched it, I'd start bleeding again. So I went back in the room, and he asked if I was ready.

"I'll let you know when I'm ready," I said.

We both got in bed and I said, "I'm not going to spend another night with you. You get out of here."

He asked one very good question: "Are you man enough to put me out?"

I wasn't, and I knew it.

This was on a Thursday night, and on Friday we went into work. I had a big patch over one eye and a cut on my lip. I was in Accounts Payable and he was right beside me in Accounts Receivable. Everybody asked me what happened. "I ran into a two-legged jackass," I told them. I promised that the next time they saw me there would either be a lot more warts on me or there would be some on him.

Over the weekend, Alan went to Charlotte, and I got out in the sun trying to dry out the cuts. It was Monday at lunchtime before I caught up with him. He went up to our room, and I asked him if he was ready to finish it. He got down in a crouch. I didn't know he took boxing in college. He got down to two feet high. How did he expect me to fight him? "You stand up and fight like a man, or I'm going to kick the hell out of you," I told him.

We broke lamps and furniture in our room and two other rooms, and after 20 minutes I had him down, but was too weak to hit him. He had a scissors hold on me but was too weak to squeeze.

"Are you ready to quit?" I asked.

"Yeah," he said.

So we quit.

In the meantime, the maid had called the police. I stretched out on the bed, and the police stopped Alan as he was leaving the boarding house and brought him back up. They asked what was going on. "We were playing," I told them. "What's the trouble?"

"Playing?" the police said.

"Yeah," I answered. "We stumbled over a few things."

They wanted to know if we could post bond. "Yeah," I said, "if my brother had any money." They wanted to know who my brother was, and I told them Brown Ketner. They asked Alan if he could post bond, and he said he could if his brother had any money. They wanted to know who Alan's brother was. When they found out he was related to Mr. Cannon, they told us to settle up with the landlady, and they got out of there. Cannon paid 100 percent of all salaries for the police.

I was so weak I couldn't move. It must have been 45 minutes or an hour later when Alan's brother came in the room and asked if he could help.

"No, I'm all right, just a little tired," I said. "How's Alan?"

He said Alan had to have three stitches in the side of his nose.

I got rejuvenated just like that. I could have run 100 yards in eight seconds. I took a shower. I got dressed. I got back to work and went right in to see Mr. Bost, the company treasurer.

"What can I do for you?" he asked.

"I had round two," I said.

"What do you mean?" he asked.

"You know what round one was last week?" I asked.

He knew all about it but didn't know what to do. Mr. Cannon hadn't called him to tell him what to do yet. He told me to go on home and if I didn't get a phone call I was to come back to work in the morning. Well, I didn't go home. I stayed away from the phone. The next morning I went into work, and Alan came in. Sybil Trexler took one look at him and jumped all over me. "The only good looking boy in this office and you did that to him?"

It's funny how things work out. I thought I'd get fired but ended up getting just what I had always wanted: a transfer to the Audit Department.

One of my first jobs as an auditor was at Cabarrus Bank and Trust Company in Kannapolis. It was owned by Cannon Mills. Six auditors looked over thousands of the bank's notes to calculate unearned interest. We had a little book with interest tables. I started doing the interest in my head. Within 45 minutes I had done about 500 of the notes, while my colleagues had done no more than 50. I asked if there were any more that I could handle.

"Just finish the ones I gave you," the boss said. I explained I had finished all of them.

He didn't like my attitude. The entire office stopped to look. One of the other auditors was assigned to check my work and found what he thought to be errors in some. He placed them in a separate stack. They were a penny off from the figure in the book of tables. I had a terrible time convincing them that the tables didn't handle fractions correctly. I was 100 percent correct, and since I could do in minutes what took hours for others, I wound up doing all the notes, literally thousands.

I had given my notice that I was quitting when Cannon's auditors were called to a subsidiary, the Ewing-Thomas Corporation in Chester, Pa. I volunteered to go. While I was there, the office manager was drafted, and I was asked to stay until a replacement could be found. In view of the fact that we received per diem, which greatly increased my salary, I volunteered.

The first night after the auditors left, I went bowling. But the entire alley was tied up with a mixed league of men and women from Baldwin Locomotive Shops. On one lane I noticed an attractive young lady on a team that was short one man. I asked if they needed a fill-in, and they asked if I worked for Baldwin Locomotive. I said yes so I could bowl.

I ended up asking the girl, Helena McFarland, for a date for the next night, and, much to my delight, she said yes. I was starting to like Pennsylvania, I told myself on the way home. The next night I caught a cab and gave the driver the address Helena had given me. It turned out to be a vacant lot.

"Take me to the bowling alley," I told the cab driver.

I went back in and verified that the girl's name was Helena McFarland and started calling all the McFarlands in the phone book. I finally got Helena and asked why she hadn't given me her real address.

She said she knew I didn't work for Baldwin Locomotive, and since I had lied about that she felt that I might be lying about wanting a date, too. I was able to convince her that I was serious, and we went out several times during the remaining weeks I spent in Chester, Pa. I'll never forget Helena McFarland because of that vacant lot.

Once I got back to Kannapolis, my job at Cannon's auditing department didn't last long. I could hear the Army calling.

3. This Man's Army

In the Army you go along to get along. If I had been able to do that, my military career would have been pretty dull. I had more battles with our own officers than I ever had with the Germans.

I can still hear President Roosevelt's voice telling America about the bombing of Pearl Harbor on Dec. 7, 1941. Knowing it was just a matter of time before I would be drafted, I volunteered for the U.S. Army in the spring of 1942 with the knowledge that our outfit would immediately be shipped overseas.

I caught a bus in May for the short trip to Monroe, North Carolina, and Camp Sutton. I don't know what I expected to see at Camp Sutton, but I sure was disappointed. The recruits had to cut trees to clear land for the tents. There were no weapons, no uniforms and no discipline. We wore our civilian clothes for weeks, and when we'd take a shower, we would just wash with our clothes on. We'd sleep as late as we wanted and wander down to the mess tent for breakfast. I'm sure there was never a sorrier looking outfit preparing to go to war than the 302nd Ordnance Battalion.

The men in the 302nd were mostly mechanics and knew automobiles and trucks. Col. Tom Wolfe, the Ford dealer in Albemarle, was commander, and it was to be our job to receive and assemble vehicles. All would be shipped to the war zone in crates, some in as many as seven or eight. The operating concept was labeled TUP-SUP: Twin Unit Pack and Single Unit Pack.

With my background in accounting and finance, I qualified for a noncommissioned officer's rating of Technician Fourth Grade or T-4, the equivalent of a buck sergeant. My job in the war zone would be to keep track of the huge inventory of chassis, axles, motors, wheels and dozens of other parts. But my job at Camp Sutton, I decided, was to do as little as possible.

But even hiding from work can be tiresome so when one of my tentmates invited me to go along to his job breaking down rations at the quartermaster depot, I agreed. At the depot, we were assigned to pick up a shipment of pork loins. Several of us were loading the meat into the truck and calling out the weights marked on the boxes for another GI to enter on an adding machine. To amuse myself, I added the numbers in my head as we went along. After all the pork had been loaded and before the GI could pull the handle on his adding machine, I told him the total — 5,238 pounds, or some such figure.

That turned out to be exactly right. My buddies were amazed. Back at company headquarters, a lieutenant who had heard about the addition feat asked me to meet a major who was in charge of the quartermaster operation. He introduced me as being in charge of ration breakdowns. The tentmate who invited me to tag along never dreamed he would be working for me before the day was out. But that's the way the Army operates. It never seemed to have rhyme or reason to me. You advanced by knowing the right people. So when I was approached by a captain from regimental supply about a new job, I transferred to his operation. It seemed that it would be better to work for a captain at regimental than a lieutenant at company headquarters.

Boy, I was right. The captain was happy with the way I did my job, which involved a lot of figuring — allocating the number of units of a supply item to each company based on the number of personnel and other computations.

One day the captain asked if there was a good laundry in Kannapolis. I assured him there was.

"Well," he asked, "why don't we ride up there every week and take our laundry? That'll give you a chance to see your friends and family and get away from here."

I thought that was a great idea. Weekend passes were no problem, and when the captain and I would visit Kannapolis, my brother Brown would send a couple of steaks back to Camp Sutton with us.

Of course, there's always somebody in the Army who wants to exercise his authority. In this case it was a sergeant who thought I was getting too many weekends off. The next time I tried to go to Kannapolis he stopped me.

"You've had six weekend passes in a row," he said, "and you're not entitled to another one."

He was right, I thought to myself. I went back to regimental headquarters to do some work and ran into the captain. He asked why I hadn't gone home, and I told him.

"Don't we need some parts around here?" the captain asked.

It didn't take too long for me to figure out what he meant.

"Yes, sir," I said. "We always need parts." The captain told me to write a letter saying that I was going into Kannapolis to look for an item that regimental supply might need. I typed the letter, the captain signed it, and I headed back toward the sergeant who wouldn't let me leave just a couple hours earlier.

"Who wrote this letter?" he demanded.

"I wrote it," I said, "but you had better look at who signed it."

The sergeant had to let me go, but revenge was just a matter of time. He got his chance in a few weeks when I asked to tie a weekend pass and a three-day pass together, giving me five days of leave. I had the three-day pass, but needed his permission to tie the two together. It was routine for most people, but he wasn't going to let me do it.

"Sarge, what if I am AWOL for an hour after my weekend pass expires?" I asked him.

"I'll throw the book at you," he said.

"Suppose I'm AWOL for 30 minutes."

"I'll still throw the book at you," he said.

"Well then, suppose I'm AWOL for just one minute."

"If you're only AWOL for one minute," he said, pausing to think, "that'll be OK."

So I left the camp on Friday afternoon with a weekend pass and a three-day pass but without permission to tie the two together. I returned five days later to find the sergeant waiting for me.

"You're in for it now, Ketner," he said. "You tied those two passes together without permission."

"No, Sarge, I didn't. I'm not stupid. You made it perfectly clear I wouldn't be allowed to do that."

"Well, when did you leave and when did you come back?" he asked.

"I left on Friday, and I just walked in a minute ago. You saw me."

"That means you put those two passes together without permission," he said.

"No I didn't, Sarge. My weekend pass ended at 5 o'clock Monday morning, and I didn't start my three-day pass until one minute past 5. I was AWOL from 5:00 to 5:01, but you said that would be all right. So what's your problem?"

The sergeant never got to throw that book at me.

I managed to avoid much of basic training — marching, close-order drill, weapons training and other instruction. But I couldn't avoid going to the rifle range for target practice. That worried me. Joining the infantry was the last thing I intended to do. My first shot missed so badly it kicked up some dirt in front of the target, but "bull's-eye" came the call.

"What the heck is going on," I thought to myself.

That's when I found out Harold Vick, an old friend of mine from Kannapolis, was calling the targets, and he intended to see that I was certified as a marksman.

"You tell Harold Vick to call 'em just the way I shoot 'em," I told the fellow manning the phone on the rifle range.

Harold went along, and called my scores as I shot them. I never could shoot.

I didn't want anything to do with the infantry. Once, in Casablanca, I was walking guard duty, and when the lieutenant came to inspect my rifle, I had no bullets. The rifle had been loaded when I started guard duty. I had not fired a shot. But the rifle was empty. We looked around and started finding bullets on the ground. I had accidentally ejected the bullets with the bolt action as I marched. In two hours I had ejected every bullet in the gun.

I didn't consider it a problem that I had skipped most of basic training, but the Army brass sure did. I had the opportunity to become an officer by taking a test while I was still at Camp Sutton. I made good grades on the written part, but in the oral examinations I really showed my ignorance. The colonel in charge asked me how I would blend two columns of men into a single column in close order drill.

"I'd have the men in back spread out and the men in front drop back," I said.

He knew right away that I had no parade ground experience and told me to go through basic training before I thought about becoming an officer.

My unit was transferred to Camp Pickett, Virginia, and I gave up my regimental job to rejoin my buddies in company headquarters. I asked for permission to drive my car, even though I didn't have one. I knew the Army paid mileage for those who drove, and I could hitchhike and collect a few extra dollars. We were only making $21 a month.

My next clash with a superior came at Fort Dix, New Jersey, in December 1942. I was in the company recreation room playing cards. When I returned to the barracks, a sergeant, who outranked me, came up and said: "Ketner, you've been AWOL."

"That's ridiculous," I said. "I was playing cards in the rec room."

He told me I didn't have authority to be out of the barracks and was AWOL.

We argued for a minute and when I couldn't take any more, I called him an SOB. The sergeant put me on kitchen police duty. That included the chore of building fires in the kitchen and outside in the early morning of a bitterly cold winter so the men would have hot water to wash their mess kits after breakfast. I didn't know anything about building a fire. I did such a bad job that breakfast was late. You can imagine how happy I was to be outside in the snow at 3 a.m. Every time I saw that sergeant I called him a little SOB. I would find myself posted for still another night on fire duty.

After four or five days, I saw that wasn't getting me anywhere. So the next time I saw him, I kept my mouth shut. I wanted off fire duty.

I thought it would be great to get back with the guys from Kannapolis, but I didn't count on running into Captain Ray. I worked in a small office with five or six other men. Captain Ray's office was a small room next to it. One day he called me into his office and said: "Ketner, I don't like your attitude." I couldn't think of any answer that wouldn't get me in more trouble, so I kept quiet. "You walk around with a smirk on your face," the captain said. "Every time I see you, you have that smirk on your face." That got me tickled and I started laughing. Dammit," the captain roared, "now you're doing it to my face. I'll have you busted if it's the last thing I ever do."

I stood there for a few more uncomfortable minutes and finally turned and walked back to my desk. The other enlisted men were laughing at me. Not wanting to let the matter drop, I got a glass of water and put it on the window ledge. Then I got a broom and leaned it against the edge of the window. That piqued everybody's attention, and they asked what I was doing. "The captain has chewed my tail out so many times that the next time he does it, I'm going to streak out of his office, get the broom, throw water on the floor, and start sweeping like the devil," I said. "When the captain asks what the hell I'm doing, I'm going to tell him he's chewed my tail out so many times that I think it's time we clean up a little bit in here."

My buddies bet me I didn't have the guts to do that, and I took some of the bets, but thank goodness Captain Ray stayed off my case until I came to my senses. That stunt could have landed me in the stockade.

Incidentally, Captain Ray never succeeded in busting me as my Company Commander refused to do so. Captain Ray had one day's seniority and had pulled rank on him. This worked to my advantage.

I was happy to ship out overseas in January 1943. Few of us knew we were heading for Casablanca in North Africa. We crossed the Atlantic as part of a big convoy, but when our ship developed engine trouble, they left us behind. That's a pretty lonely feeling, being in a single boat in the ocean. We were afraid that a German submarine might spot us, but the crew got the engines repaired in a few hours and we rejoined the convoy.

Some of the guys heard that they could trade trinkets with the natives and took tubes of lipstick and things like that with them. I thought that Casablanca was going to be a jungle. It was a modern city. My first night there I was paired with another fellow, and we were given a pup tent to erect. "I sure hope you know how to put up this thing," I told him. "I was hoping you knew," he said. We used the tent like a blanket and slept on the ground that first night and nearly froze.

I was working in regimental supply when Lt. J. J. Barnhardt asked me to join his section keeping track of incoming TUP-SUP shipments. I knew Lt. Barnhardt from Cannon Mills, where his father was a vice president. He had heard about my ability with figures.

I jumped at the chance to work for him, figuring it would be to my advantage to work with a guy from home. Our responsibility was to take individual receipts for shipments coming into the TUP-SUP each day and compile a report for the general in command of supply and ordnance in the Casablanca area. The report would describe the vehicle parts that arrived and the number of complete units that could be assembled from parts on hand.

It took five enlisted men and Lt. Barnhardt to compile the TUP-SUP report, posting individual hand-written listings for 10 or 15 different parts, each on a separate page. The inventories of those parts — 50 or 75 different types all told — had to be incorporated into the daily report. There had to be an easier way.

I designed a form that listed all the vehicle parts, and the receivers simply made a mark in the right space. I took the form to Lt. Barnhardt. Unlike a lot of other officers, he was receptive to ideas no matter where they came from. Once we started using the form, things went so smoothly and efficiently that one man could do the whole job that once had taken five enlisted men and an officer. Lt. Barnhardt went to Colonel Wolfe and told him he was no longer needed. "Ralph Ketner is able to do everything by himself, and I would appreciate your reassigning me." The lieutenant got his request and the four enlisted men working with me were also reassigned, leaving me to run the operation alone.

Since Colonel Wolfe paid little attention to the daily reports on the TUP-SUP parts, I decided to save him some time and sign them myself. One day, after I had been working this one-man job for several weeks, I heard the colonel on the telephone: "Yes, sir! Yes, sir!" From what he was saying and the tone of his voice, I figured the colonel was talking to a general and as soon as he got off the phone somebody was going to catch it. I didn't realize it was going to be me.

"Ketner, who in the hell has been signing that report that you turn in each morning to General Slaughter?"

"I have, sir," I said. "I've been signing it for weeks. Since you didn't look at it, I figured I would save you some time."

"Well, General Slaughter doesn't want any reports coming across his desk signed by a sergeant," Colonel Wolfe said.

"Fine, sir. From now on I'll route the report directly to you for you to sign."

That made the general happy — and that made me happy.

My system of keeping track of parts worked so well that I had a lot of spare time. I finished by 2 o'clock most afternoons and would go to the movies or some place. George Stovall, the outfit's chief clerk, who had been Colonel Wolfe's bookkeeper in civilian life, got concerned over where I was going every afternoon. I told him the truth, but he thought I was doing something sinister. I should have known something was up when George sent me an assistant, Dan Reed. I had been asking for somebody, because there was nobody who could do the job if I got sick. My requests had been hitting a brick wall before George's curiosity got aroused.

I followed the same routine with Dan that I had on my own, finishing the work in the early- or mid-afternoon and then going into town for some recreation. Dan tagged along a few times and then asked me what we were going to tell George. "Just tell him the truth," I said. "That's what I've been doing all along."

After we both had been reassigned, I learned that Dan had been sent to spy on me so George Stoval could get me in trouble. I was lucky that Dan was an honest man because he could have made up any wild tale and George would have believed it.

I thought I deserved some recognition for designing a TUP-SUP form that allowed one man to do the work of five enlisted men and one officer. When I learned that every battalion was entitled to at least one Legion of Merit medal for a man who had accomplished meritorious service, I let my superiors know that I felt qualified. Did I get it? No. Who did? Somebody who dug latrines for the officers.

Dugan Aycock, a golf pro from Lexington, built a nine-hole golf course for the officers and got promoted just like that. Six stripes. A crazy thing. I made up my mind right there that I would just count the days until I could get out of this man's army.

I left the 302nd Ordnance Battalion to join the fiscal department of the Atlantic Base headquarters during my time in Casablanca, most of 1943. It seemed like such a good opportunity for advancement, I accepted a reduction in rank from sergeant to corporal, figuring I could earn back the lost stripe and add more. I didn't know much about the Army.

My new job was to assist a master sergeant who was auditing all quartermaster sales officers, officers clubs and similar areas. My sergeant had a run-in with the operation's commanding officer, Col. James Carter, and was transferred. That left Corporal Ketner in charge of the department. That was fine with me. I enjoyed the work, but promotions proved harder to get than I had expected and it was quite a while before I was a sergeant again.

Every time I turned around, there seemed to be something crazy happening to me. The exchange rate in Casablanca was 75 francs to the dollar, but overnight the rate went to 50. I owed this fellow $50 from poker, but he said that I now owed him $75 because if he had the money he could have converted his dollars to francs. And the colonel backed him up and said that I owed him $75. Using that logic, I said, "He might have lost the money playing cards, and I don't owe him anything." But I paid the $75.

In September 1943, Allied troops invaded Italy, and in October the Germans left Naples. My outfit moved into the city two days later — several days too soon as far as I was concerned. Our headquarters unit occupied the eighth floor of an office building. The elevators were reserved for officers, and the enlisted men had to carry boxes of financial records up seven flights of stairs. Fortunately, there were Italian men begging for work at any price. We paid them with cigarettes and chocolate bars to help us lug the boxes up the stairs.

Two days after we arrived, a booby trap exploded in the post office where we were bivouacked. I was on the eighth floor of the finance building when I heard the blast. The Germans had rigged a can to a wire and when the can filled with rain water, the wire tripped the bomb in the basement. There were 20 or 30 civilian deaths but none in my outfit. It was probably the closest I came to the shooting war.

While I was in Italy, I learned how to win at poker. I had been losing for months, and one day while doing an audit I said to myself that anybody with my knack for figures ought to be able to play poker. I sent off for a book, and, brother, I learned that book backward and forward. I'd win 29 nights out of 30. I'm still a lousy poker player. A good poker player studies mannerisms and facial expressions. He can read your face and tell whether you have good cards. I'm a good percentage player. I didn't drink. They did. I didn't play hunches. They did. I played strictly mathematics. I can tell you the odds of drawing any card out of any deck under any conditions. I didn't win much, maybe $50 to $75 a night. Everybody else tried to make a killing: win $500. Of course, they lost $500 some nights too. But if six people played poker like I did, everybody would quit in 15 minutes.

I won so much I had to ask permission from the colonel to send money home. You had to get permission because of the black marketers. They would send 100 times their salary home and the Army wanted to stop it. The colonel gave me permission to send the money to my stepmother. "Ketner, you make more than I do," he said.

"Sir, I work a lot harder than you do. I'm up every night until 2 o'clock playing poker and I get up at 5 or 6 every morning."

I offered to send my brother Brown $250 a month, if he would quit Glenn's store and become a comedian, like Bob Hope. All I wanted to do when I got out of service was to be his manager. He was going to resign, but one night he was in a restaurant and asked somebody with three stripes — he knew that's what I had — how much money he made. I think it was maybe $110 a month. He got nervous about my promising him $250 a month, but he didn't know about my new poker skill.

That's not to say my time in Naples was pleasant. Warrant Officer Chester D. Flanders did all he could to make my life miserable. A warrant officer is superior to a non-commissioned officer and inferior to a commissioned officer. They were addressed as "Mister" and I often found it hard to use that term of respect.

My first run-in with Mr. Flanders, who supervised four enlisted men in the office, came after I proposed doing an audit of salvage officers. Mr. Flanders listened but didn't have a great deal to say about the idea. Several days later Colonel Carter walked into our offices.

"Sergeant," he said to me, "Mr. Flanders has what I think is an excellent idea regarding the need on our part to be auditing the salvage officer's account."

For nearly a half hour, I let the colonel explain to me what was my own idea. Then, knowing the enlisted men in the office were aware the idea was mine, I said to the colonel, "Sir, when Mr. Flanders told you about MY idea, did he explain I would need one extra man to do the job?"

Sensing the truth, the colonel diplomatically excused himself. Mr. Flanders also found a reason to leave. Several days later the colonel called me into his office. "Ketner," he said, "your idea is quite good and I think we ought to audit the salvage officers' accounts. But I've been checking on it, and the accounts only amount to about $500,000 a month. So it isn't worth our time and trouble to try and audit them now."

That was the most casual attitude I've ever come across toward half a million dollars a month.

Mr. Flanders spent the next six months trying to get even with me for embarrassing him in front of the colonel. He ordered me to drive him when he wanted to go to the Officers Club or a social function. I would have to wait outside in the Jeep. Finally, I got fed up and tore my driver's license into shreds right in front of his face. When he asked what I was doing, I told him that not having a license, I would no longer be able to drive him. That worked for a couple of weeks, but he ordered me to drive him to an evening function and there I was — Chester Flanders' personal chauffeur again. I hoped that I would be stopped by the military police, and they would learn that I was driving without a license.

That never happened, but I did finally get some measure of revenge. My unit was transferred to Leghorn, Italy, north of Rome. I was assigned CQ (in charge of quarters) duty which required me to carry a pistol. The following morning, when I was relieved, the pistol was missing. Mr. Flanders sensed an opportunity to cause some serious trouble for me and said he was going to do a survey for the pistol. If the survey proved me responsible for the pistol, I would have to pay for it.

I suspected that somebody had stolen the pistol during the night, but when I checked the record I found that I hadn't signed for it and truthfully never recall seeing it. The last name on the pistol sheet: Chester Flanders. He had signed for the pistol the day before.

"Mr. Flanders," I said, "when you survey the missing pistol, be sure to spell the name of the person being surveyed correctly."

"I know how to spell Ketner: K-e-t-n-e-r," he replied.

"I believe you're making a mistake," I told him. "I think the correct spelling is F-l-a-n-d-e-r-s." Then I explained that his name was the last on the record as having received the pistol. I had not signed for it the previous night and could not be held responsible. There was no further mention of any survey.

Even though it sounds like my military career was one long confrontation with my superior officers, I have some wonderful memories and made some good friends. While I was stationed in Leghorn, Italy, I had the opportunity to go to a beach resort for some R and R (rest and relaxation). I overheard one of the Red

Cross ladies mention that there would be a performance that evening where the GI's would be encouraged to participate. The prize was a beautiful homemade cake. I could practically taste that cake. I told my tentmates about the contest and my plan: Five of us would sit on the front row and when they asked for volunteers, we would jump up. One of us would have to win the cake, and we would all share the prize.

Everything went as planned until the lady asked for volunteers. I jumped up, but my four friends stayed in their seats, laughing at the trick they had pulled on me. I couldn't back out. I was able to answer the questions and was one of the finalists. I was asked to name a number of songs with girls' names in the titles. I got them all but one, and I thought of "Gypsy."

"I don't know of anyone named Gypsy," said the lady in charge.

"How about Gypsy Rose Lee?" I asked.

"I can tell what you are thinking about," she said, "but I will have to let that one count. You are the winner of the cake."

Naturally, I shared it with my buddies, and we all had a big laugh.

I had fun with the guys in my unit. We were always playing tricks on each other. One day somebody ordered me to move a big box to the supply room, and I asked a couple of the fellows for help. The box was too heavy for one person to carry. They wouldn't help me, but one skinny, little guy said he could carry it. I bet him a dollar or two, and the little jackass picked it up and put it on the porch. "I mean inside the store room," I said. "You didn't do what we bet." But I knew that I had lost the bet, and the guys were protesting that I owed him. I slipped over so no one could see and pushed a couple of dollars in his hand to settle the bet.

"Anybody who wants to say I owe him, put up or shut up," I announced. They wanted to know who would decide. "We'll let him decide," I said, pointing to the little guy. "He knows if I owe him or not." I made a few $5 bets and then asked if I owed him any money. "No, Ralph, paid me a few minutes ago," the little guy told them. I did some things I probably shouldn't be proud of.

I spent a night in jail in Venice. And I was glad to be there.

It all began when I had a weekend pass to Naples, and I went to the airport but couldn't catch a ride. I asked one pilot where he was going. "France," he yelled over the engine noise. I didn't have that kind of guts, but when I changed my mind, I couldn't get his attention.

I found a pilot going to Rome, and when I got there I caught a ride to Florence, Italy. There was a plane revving up there, so I jumped in without asking where he was heading. It turned out to be Venice, a town off limits to American troops. Only British were supposed to be there, and I couldn't find a hotel room. An Italian saw that I had a problem and offered to help. We were walking in the worst section of town, and I started to think that my bag was filled with cigarettes — that was the medium of exchange — and I might not be in the right place. I got back to the center of town, and I was ready to sleep on the concrete when two British Red Cross workers asked me if I would mind spending the night in the jail. They took me to the police station, and I got a bunk and a good night's sleep. I gave them all packs of cigarettes when I left the next day. I slipped on a plane without a pass and got home before my weekend pass expired. The colonel couldn't believe where I had been. "You mean you went to Venice and I can't?" he roared. I've always been willing to take a chance.

When the war in Europe ended we were subject to reassignment for service in the Pacific. I had a hernia, so I put in for limited service status, just to make sure that I didn't get too close to the shooting. That made the colonel mad and he ordered me to report to the hospital right away. He thought he was calling my bluff. But I had a really bad hernia, and the doctor told me to go into a room to get ready for an operation the next day. I had to do some fast talking. I didn't want the hernia fixed. I wanted to be able to use it as an excuse for the rest of my time in the Army. "The colonel just wants to know that I have a hernia," I explained to the doctor. "Just write me a note."

The doctor wanted to do the surgery, but I left and reported back to the colonel.

"What did he say?" the colonel wanted to know.

"He said to just take real good care of it," I told him.

When the war in Europe had ended and the American Fifth Army was pulling out, the colonel who had considered auditing the salvage officers' accounts months before called me in again. "Ketner," he asked, "why haven't we been auditing the salvage officers' accounts?" I reminded him I had proposed doing that, and he had decided there wasn't enough money involved to make it worthwhile. Now, with the Fifth Army leaving, my Peninsula Base Headquarters had to take over a lot of Fifth Army functions, including auditing.

That put the matter in my lap. I studied the procedure Fifth Army had used to audit salvage officers' accounts and found that it left a lot to be desired. Fifth Army's audit consisted of comparisons of the sales reported by the salvage officer and a report turned in by the bank, acknowledging the money he turned in. The procedure assumed that if the salvage officer attempted to steal any money, it would be after he turned it in to the bank. However, any funds that might have been misappropriated prior to making the banking deposit would never have been discovered. Sounds stupid — was stupid.

The colonel and I decided it was too late to change things. We would both be going home in a short time.

After the war ended, a system of points was instituted to set priorities on who got to go home first. The system was based on the number of months an individual had been overseas, whether he was married and had dependents, how many combat zones he had served in and other factors.

Like most GIs, I was anxious to return to civilian life as soon as possible. I found that I could earn another five points toward the 85 needed to get out if I received a certain battle star. Those who crossed the Arno River near Florence between certain dates qualified. Our outfit hadn't crossed the river, but I had when I went to audit the quartermaster depot in Florence.

My commanding officer, Col. Carter, didn't take kindly to my request for the star and the points. Though I was technically qualified, the colonel didn't think I deserved the star and would not recommend that I get it. I was prepared to pursue the matter when the number of points needed for rotation was dropped. There was no reason to keep pushing for the battle star. I was going home.

In late 1945, I shipped out of Naples for home. I had been overseas almost three years and thought nothing could spoil the voyage. But that's the Army for you. I was wrong again.

I was made first sergeant of a group of Army GIs and had to learn a long list of regulations. That served me well because it didn't take long for me to find a poker game in crew quarters. The major in charge of the ship, accompanied by a lieutenant, came into the quarters, pointed at the soldiers in our poker game and ordered them placed in the brig on bread and water for the rest of the trip.

At first I wondered what the others had done to deserve this treatment. I didn't realize that I was under arrest, too. When the officers told me I had violated regulations by gambling and being in the quarters of the Merchant Marine crewmen, I was able to point out that there was nothing in the regulations that prohibited us from going into crew quarters. And the major himself had declared over the ship's public address system that gambling would be permitted if no pots were cut. Since there had been no cutting, I told the officers, none of us had done anything wrong.

The major and the lieutenant had no choice but to back down. But I knew that I'd better watch my step the rest of the way home.

I mustered out of service at Fort Bragg, North Carolina. I didn't want to leave without getting my hernia corrected. By then it was late November 1945, and I talked my way into a weekend pass to go home for Thanksgiving before the operation. When I got back, I talked my way into a Christmas leave before surgery. I went into the operating room in January 1946. I spent 14 days in pain flat on my back. I found that I had no use for bedpans. On the 13th day I tried to get up to use the bathroom and thought my stomach was falling through my feet. After I recuperated, I happily became private citizen Ralph Ketner after nearly four years of military service.

After I was discharged from the U.S. Army in 1946, I joined the Harold B. Jarrett American Legion Post in Salisbury, N.C., which met in a building on Klumac Road at the time. Shortly after I joined, they raffled off a new Oldsmobile to raise money to build a new home for their club. This was successful, and the money was deposited in the bank awaiting a decision as to when and where to build. I moved to San Francisco in early 1948 and returned in September that same year.

The first meeting I attended of the Harold B. Jarrett Post, upon my return from California, the main point of discussion was how to get their funds out of the bank in order to build a new facility on Lincolnton Road. It developed that when the money was deposited, it was done so upon a motion by the members that it required a vote of two-thirds of the members present and voting in favor of same. During the approximately seven months that I had been missing from Salisbury, they had attempted time after time to get two-thirds of the members to attend the meeting but without success. The meeting I was attending at that time was the largest group they had ever had, but even then they fell short of the two-thirds required in order to move the monies.

Upon hearing this discussion, I asked the Commander to read again the motion which originally deposited the funds received from the Oldsmobile raffle. He did, and, basically, the motion was that it required a two-thirds vote of the outstanding membership in order to move the monies from the bank account. I asked the number of members we had, and the figure, I believe, was 118. I then said that it would be impossible to meet this requirement and, therefore, the motion as made could be declared unconstitutional and, therefore, void. They asked what I was talking about.

"Two-thirds of 118 is 78 2/3," I said. "I feel certain that no member is going to be willing to dismember himself to the extent that he qualified as a two-thirds member.

They immediately said, "Well, you know that the motion means two-thirds or more.

I reminded them that the motion did not have the words "or more" in it, therefore, it did not mean "or more." I said, "If the teacher asked me what two-thirds of 75 was, and I knew the answer was 50, but I said 74, do you think I would get 100 from the teacher? Obviously, there is only one correct answer, that being 50. Therefore, in my opinion, they should adjourn for a few minutes and let the Executive Committee vote on my argument as to whether the motion of putting the funds in under the ambiguous wording was in order."

They decided that perhaps my way out was the only way out. Therefore, they did call a recess, returning in a couple of minutes stating that they felt the original motion made was in error, therefore if those members present voted in favor of removing the funds and starting the building project, that it would be done immediately. This was the net outcome. They now have a beautiful building on Lincolnton Road here in Salisbury. I often wonder if it had not been for my being at that particular meeting and coming up with the solution, whether those funds would still be sitting in the bank and the Harold B. Jarrett American Legion would still be meeting in a building off Klumac Road.

A pleasant postscript to my military service was added to my life a few years ago when my wife, Anne, and I had a reunion with four of my closest buddies from the Army, men I had been associated with in the fiscal department at Casablanca, Naples and Leghorn: Ollie Olson, Cecil Germany, Don Moriarity and Joe Schultz.

I had come across a photo of us made in 1943. The men's hometowns were written on the back of the photo, and I was able to find addresses for three of the four. But I couldn't locate Ollie Olson of Detroit Lakes, Minnesota. After sending letters and making other inquiries, I called the telephone operator in Detroit Lakes. She had no listing for Ollie Olson, but asked if his name could be Orvis Olson? Yes, that was it. The operator knew Ollie well; he worked in the building next to hers and within minutes I was speaking with him.

Anne and I invited the four of them and their wives to meet us for a reunion in Las Vegas at our expense. Everything was arranged, and we met at the Desert Inn. One evening, a female photographer snapped a shot of us all and went out to have it developed and printed. My wife slipped out a few seconds later and gave the photographer enlarged copies of the old Army photo from 1943 she had brought with her. The photographer came back with a broad smile on her face.

"You know, you fellows really do show up young in your pictures," she said. Then she passed out the enlarged shots of the photo taken in Naples 40 years earlier.

We had a wonderful time. My wife said later that we talked as though we'd been apart 40 minutes instead of 40 years. The Army never seemed so good.

4. Nine Jobs I Didn't Like

I tried everything under the sun to stay out of the grocery business. I worked in Kannapolis, San Francisco, Atlanta, Philadelphia, Charlotte and Raleigh and took a test for a job in Saudi Arabia. When it was all over, I had found nine things that I didn't want to do.

If you've ever been rabbit hunting, you know that when the rabbit takes off he'll make a circle and eventually come right back. That's where the hunters wait. I must have looked like a scared rabbit myself in the late '40s. I went to work for Glenn as soon as I got out of the Army and jumped all around the country in various jobs before I came full circle. But I learned a lot along the way.

After the war Glenn formed Excel Grocery Company, a warehouse operation to supply his seven retail stores. He must have had quite a bit of confidence in me, because he put me in charge and started teaching me the grocery business from the ground up.

It was considered impossible to get on "direct" with suppliers. Excel was small potatoes to many of the cigarette and candy manufacturers, but we needed to buy directly from them rather than go through a jobber. The more people who handle a product the more expensive it becomes. Glenn wanted me to write the companies, mention my years of military service and ask them to make an exception. That worked with some, but most of the companies sent me a form letter that said they wouldn't do it. Discouraged, I asked Glenn what to do.

"Write them again," he said. "Keep hammering away at them. Don't take no for an answer."

I wrote as many as five letters to some cigarette companies explaining that I hadn't spent 45 months in the Army to be turned down on a legitimate proposition like this. Little by little, they relented and we went on every direct cigarette wholesale list except one. Glenn solved that problem. He drew up an advertisement listing that company's prices 20 to 30 cents higher than other brands. No company wants to look bad in comparison with competitors, and eventually that last holdout came around to our way of thinking.

Working until 9 and 10 o'clock in Glenn's warehouse was cutting into my new-found social life. I had a brand new Oldsmobile but nowhere to go. A new car was hard to come by in those days, but my brother Brown had some connections in Kannapolis. I used the poker winnings I had sent home from the war to pay for it. But what good was it doing me if I had to wait around a grocery warehouse half the night on late delivery trucks?

After about six months, I said good-bye to the grocery business and took a job with Central Motor Lines in Kannapolis as assistant office manager and auditor. Cannon Mills owned the trucking line because of a fear that a strike would shut down the railroads, and it wouldn't be able to ship its products. The people at Cannon Mills knew that I would question every procedure in the books, and I didn't disappoint them.

Payments made in cash to Central Motor Lines were treated differently from payments made by check. If 100 deliveries were made at a charge of $5 each and payments were made in cash, the transaction was treated as a debit cash entry for $500 and credit revenue for $500. If the same 100 deliveries were paid for by check, each individual entry would be posted as an account receivable. The checks would have to work their way through the bookkeeping process to offset the debit created when the invoices were posted as accounts receivable. It required far too many entries.

"Checks are as negotiable as cash," I told my boss, but every time I raised a question he would throw a question at me about accounting in the trucking business that I didn't understand. I would go home and study the procedures and come back with new questions the next day. Finally, I had an argument he couldn't beat. I studied all the checks over a 30-day period — 14,400 transactions — and told him I could eliminate 14,000 if he would give me the chance.

The boss took the matter to Mr. Willer, head of the Cannon Mills auditing department. He remembered that I had worked for him before the war, but I'm not sure that helped my case. He pointed out the procedures at Central Motor Lines had been used for 15 years without being questioned.

After a half-hour of discussion, Mr. Willer told me, "Ralph, I know you're not going to give up unless we do it your way."

"But Mr. Willer, my way is the correct way," I said.

"Okay," he said, "we'll try it. But if it doesn't work we'll know who talked us into it."

My way did work and resulted in cutting a tremendous number of postings and payroll expenses. Eventually the company was able to eliminate about 10 positions in the accounting department because of that improvement and several others I proposed.

I married Ruth Jones on Aug. 1, 1947. Central Motor Lines helped us go on a honeymoon. There was a terminal in Chicago that needed an audit, so I convinced them to send me up there and I could tie it in with my honeymoon. They would pay mileage, and we would drive by Flint, Michigan, where Ruth had some friends, and then on to Chicago, where I did the audit.

We didn't know where we were going to live when we got married, but Jim Glover, my stepmother's brother, had a home out from town on Old Concord Road. He offered to rent it to us lock, stock and barrel. The Glovers wanted to move to Florida and left the bedclothes, towels, groceries in the cupboard, everything. We came back to a ready-made place to live.

Ruth had lived in San Francisco during the war and had met Jim and Wanda Kelly. Jim worked for the Army Exchange Service, and they wrote to tell us they were coming to Atlanta and would like to visit us for a weekend. They came and I told him how Central Motor Lines was doing so many things that wasted money and the changes I had made. Jim asked me how much money I made, and I told him.

"How would you like to have a job paying double that?" he asked.

I said I'd take it quicker than he could bat an eye.

I thought he was shooting the bull, but in two weeks I got a letter saying that if I wanted the job to call a number in San Francisco immediately — don't write, don't wire. I had to go next door to use their phone as we couldn't afford one.

"We were ready to hire you until we found out Jim had only known you two days," he said. "We can't hire anybody to head this department on two days of Jim's recommendation. Would you go to Atlanta for an interview?"

I agreed and took some tests in Atlanta. In two weeks he called back and said if I could be in San Francisco in two weeks, the job was mine. But I had the same problem that hounded me for over two-thirds of my life: I had no money.

We were friends with Paige and Mary Ida Hess and knew they had been planning to get married as soon as Mary Ida's divorce was final.

"Why don't you two get married Tuesday at noon, just as soon as Mary Ida's divorce is final, and go along with us to San Francisco?" I asked them. "Everybody out there is looking for people to work. You're a welder, Paige, and you can get a job in nothing flat." They decided it was a good idea.

They agreed to pay for the gas. We stopped the first night in Atlanta for them to have a honeymoon. The next night we were in Texas, and I figured we'd be in San Francisco the next night. That's a big state, Texas. It took a little longer than I figured, but we finally got there and found a big room at a boarding house that had been used in the old movie "I Remember Mama" with Irene Dunne. We stayed there two nights before the girls found a nice place with two bedrooms, a living room and a kitchen. I thought I had just enough money to swing it before I found out we had to have the first and last month in advance. I didn't have it. Paige didn't either, but he could write home for some money. I didn't have anyone I thought would send me $75. I knew I was in trouble.

I went back to the office that day, and one of the girls in my department asked me when I was going to turn in my expense account. She said the company pays a per diem for coming out here from North Carolina.

"Let's talk a little bit," I said.

She explained the company pays expenses, even shipping — we had shipped our belongings out before we left. We figured that I had $300 coming, but it would take about three weeks to get the check.

"In an extreme emergency, how long does it take?" I asked.

She said I could have it the next day.

The Lord was still looking out for me.

We moved into that apartment and took up residence in the City By the Bay. The work in the budgetary figures department proved challenging. It was my job to get the figures from the eight Army Exchanges in the Pacific states. We were all civilians except for one colonel. Sometimes it was helpful to have rank on your side. I had one report that didn't come in. I kept calling. On Thursday the guy said he had mailed it Wednesday. I called on Friday, and the guy said he had mailed in Wednesday. I called on Saturday, and he said, "I told you I mailed it Wednesday." I said that it hadn't arrived and asked if he would give me the figures over the phone.

"If you would quit calling and aggravating me," he said, "I'd have time to finish the damn thing."

"Just a minute, Major," I said. "You want to talk to the colonel."

The colonel got on the phone. "Major," he said, "you've got 30 minutes to put some figures together. I don't care where they come from as long as you get them. I don't care whether you make them up out of thin air. But you're going to give Ketner some answers."

I had told my wife that I would probably work late that night, but I ended up working all night. We didn't have a telephone, so I couldn't call to tell her I wouldn't be home. About 2 o'clock in the morning Paige called from an all-night place, worried to death something had happened to me.

The head man of all the Army Exchanges came out to see me because I was the new boy on the block. He wanted me to go to Chicago and see so-and-so.

"He's the best in the business in your job," he told me. They had this new form, the most unwieldy thing I had ever seen. So I started trying to figure out a way to do it better. And I did. I made it about one-fifth the size. It gave the same answers. It would have been perfect, except for one thing: The guy in Chicago had developed the old form. I'd been up there a couple of days when he asked me about learning his form.

"Yeah, I got one before I left San Francisco," I said, "but I devised a new one that's a lot better than yours."

"What?" he said.

"Yeah," I answered.

He didn't want to see mine that first day, but eventually asked to see it and then began trying to tear it apart. I said, "Look, I'm not trying to sell it to you, I don't care if you use it or not. I'm gong to use it in San Francisco."

Some people just have too much pride. I could do it in one-third the time, but it's human nature to resist change. I love change.

I got back to San Francisco and did something I never thought I would do in my whole life: apply to become an officer in the U.S. Army Reserve. The colonel asked if I was in the Reserves and I answered that I was a tech sergeant.

"I've got to get you to be a lieutenant," the Colonel said.

"Sir, I don't want to be a lieutenant. Nothing personal, I don't want to be an officer." I was talking to a colonel and had to be careful.

"Let me put it to you this way," the colonel said. "If they call you for duty in Korea, I can't keep you here as a sergeant. As a lieutenant, you don't have to leave this office."

"Where do I go to see about becoming a lieutenant?" I asked. I took the examination and became a second lieutenant and eventually became a first lieutenant without ever going to a meeting.

Ruth's father was in poor health, and she wanted to come back to North Carolina. I had taken an examination to become an Internal Revenue Agent and got a letter from Jim Ketner (no relation) offering me a job as a CAF 5. I passed the exam for a CAF 7 and told him that I would like to come back as a 7, not as a 5. He called back and said he could do that. So I gave my notice at the Army Exchange. In the meantime, I had read that they were hiring accountants in Saudi Arabia at double what I was making. I took the exam and waited for them to call with a job. Four or five days passed so I went to see them. "Why didn't I hear from you?" I asked. "I know I passed the examination."

"We can't hire you," I was told. "You made too high on the test: a 99."

They said they didn't hire anybody who had over an 80 on the test because some other company would hire them as soon as they got to Saudi Arabia, and they would have the expense of sending them over there.

"Let me take the exam again," I said. "I can make 80 just as easily as 99." They wouldn't let me.

I came back to North Carolina and became a federal revenue agent, and the first pay I got was as a CF5. I went to Mr. Ketner.

"That's not right," he said.

"I know that's not right," I said.

He called Washington and was told all the CF7 positions were allotted, and I would have to remain a 5 until an opening came up. It could be three months, six months. They didn't know.

In the meantime, the Army Exchange, the same outfit I had worked for in San Francisco, offered me a job in Atlanta. So I quit after just one month. I just hated Atlanta. The office wasn't like the San Francisco operation at all, and when Bill Pollock, an old Army buddy from Leghorn, Italy, wanted me to come to Philadelphia to work for his family business I quit again — this time after only two weeks. He told me in the Army that I could become treasurer of his family's manufacturing appraisal business. Atlanta is the only place I never gave notice. I just didn't show up for work on Monday. I didn't wait for the money. I didn't want anything. Bill said his job was waiting for me.

Ruth and I drove from Atlanta, and I dropped her off in Faith where her dad ran a little store, Jones Grocery. I started work in Philadelphia and looked for an apartment. The only one I could afford was in the worst part of town. It had a pull-down bed, a little efficiency kitchen. It wasn't much of a place. And the job wasn't for me either. The one job I went on was the appraisal of the Ben Franklin Hotel in Philadelphia. We were supposed to count everything in every room: one desk, one chair, one bed, and describe them. They had an art critic who could look at paintings and tell whether they were real or not. I was trying to look like I knew what was going on, but they kept calling out "one chiffonier," and I said, "What is a chiffonier?" He pointed at one.

"You're talking about a dresser," I said. "That's what we call them where I come from."

It didn't take me long, about three weeks, to decide I didn't belong there. I was taking money under false pretenses. "This thing's over my head," I told Bill. "I don't know what they're talking about."

Bill said, "I want you for a figure man. I just thought you'd get the experience."

"You know I'm not going to like working in Philadelphia," I said. I worked six weeks and quit. Bill, asked me what I was going to do. I had an idea, one that I had been wanting to try since I was a kid and selling *The New York News* and "Dick Tracy" and *The New York Mirror* and "Joe Palooka" comics. If I could get boys in Salisbury to deliver these papers once a week, they would make as much as they would make for delivering *The Salisbury Post* seven days a week. I thought most people would buy the comics for 10 or 15 cents.

"I'm going to New York," I told Bill, "to try and convince those people to let me be their distributor."

Bill knew the circulation manager for *The New York News* and wrote a personal letter for me. I went up there and explained what I wanted to do.

"It won't work," he said. "We won't do it."

I told him I was going to *The New York Mirror* and see if they would to it.

"If he does it, you let me know," the News man said.

The New York Mirror thought it was a great idea, and they agreed to ship them to me. I went back to The News, and he said "How many do you want?" I decided on 3,000 copies. I had 2,000 of *The Mirror*, and I came back to Salisbury ready to set up for business. I went to the schools and asked for four or five kids who were needy and laid out routes around Salisbury and Kannapolis. I thought I was all set for the newspapers, but I found out they wouldn't ship them off the main road to Jones Grocery in Faith. The Spur gas station on North Main agreed to take the papers for me. I didn't know they came in four sections. So when I went to pick them up, I had 5,000 units of four separate sections: 20,000 different parts of paper that had to be assembled. My wife and I worked Saturday and Sunday nights. I took the papers around to the boys on Monday so they could begin delivering them. On Wednesday, I went to check on them and some hadn't even cut the string on the bundles. They hadn't even read the funny papers. I knew I was in trouble then. The ones who had worked sold out. It was a great idea, but I could see that it wasn't going to work. I called the newspapers and said. "For God's sake, don't ship me any more." The Mirror asked what had happened, and I told them that I was only going to sell 1,000 or 1,200 at most. They said that was great.

"Not when you leave 2,000 and don't make any money," I said. I convinced my brother Glenn to help sell them in his stores. He made me give him a discount, but that was better than eating them myself. My newspaper career was a one-week thing that didn't work.

After the newspaper debacle, I got a job as an auditor with the North Carolina Department of Revenue in the franchise tax division. I told Ruth we were moving to Raleigh.

The best way for me to learn something is to see what the other guy did, so I looked over an account and saw it was wrong. I ran it again and found it wrong again. I told the boss, and he said "Don't say it's wrong, because your predecessor did it, and he was the best we've ever had."

I went back to the desk and did it again — and it was still wrong. "This is one of two things," I told the boss. "Either the other guy didn't know what he was doing or I don't know what I'm doing. If I don't know what I'm doing, you ought to fire me. The guy's all wrong. Hickory Telephone company owes us $9,000."

"Well, why don't you write and tell them they owe us then," the boss said.

And I did. In about three weeks the boss received a three page letter from Hickory Telephone. He looked it over and asked me what I thought it said.

"It's three pages meant to confuse you," I told him. "They still owe us $9,000."

The North Carolina Department of Revenue paid its agents if they attend an Army Reserve Camp. I had never attended one, but being a second lieutenant in the Army Reserve as a result of having received a promotion while working for the Army Exchange in San Francisco, I decided that the additional income would be well worth the effort. I went to Fort Bragg for two weeks and was assigned to work with the base auditor. Another reservist there was an IRS agent from Greensboro. I spent several days working with the woman who was auditing one of the officers' clubs. She completed what she called an audit and was typing the results when I asked "When do you plan to start the audit?"

"What do you think we have been doing for the past three or four days?" she answered.

"I've been wondering all the time but felt you would tell me sooner or later," I said. "We have not made an audit. All you have done is accept the figures given to you by the officer in charge of the Officers Club. If you want to make an audit, you must convert all purchases to retail and extend the quantity purchased by the selling price to determine the amount of money that should be accounted for. That is the only way that you could really tell what was short. The method that you have been using works strictly from a cost standpoint, and it is impossible to determine the shortage."

The reservist who was an IRS agent said it would take weeks to convert all purchases of beer, cigarettes, candy and other items from cost to retail.

I told him I believed I could do as many as 100 in five minutes. He wanted to bet money that I couldn't do it. I didn't want to take unfair advantage of him, so we just bet a round of drinks for the office. I quickly converted the numbers, won the bet and found that the Officers Club was short a considerable amount of money. Later the auditor mentioned to me that the inspector general had discovered her previous audits were improperly done, but he had never explained how to do them correctly. The woman at the base was most appreciative of being told the right way to do an audit, but I found that she wasn't the only auditor who failed to challenge the figures.

After returning to Raleigh, it didn't take long for me to start getting bored. I told my boss that any fool could do this job. "As long as the figures add up, the auditors don't question a thing. You don't need me. You just need somebody with an adding machine, if you're not going to question them. "

I told him I was quitting unless he transferred me to the field.

He sent me to Charlotte, and the first thing they gave me was Hickory Telephone Co. to do the first field audit in the history of the franchise tax division. Nobody had ever audited an account in the field. In Raleigh, they called it an audit, but all they did was add figures. The only way they would ever find an error was if somebody made an error in arithmetic. I asked the head man, Sam Pruden, how I was supposed to do the audit.

"You'll be the first," he said. "We can't tell you how to do it."

I went to Hickory Telephone and in two or three days came up with the same figure: $9,000. The fellow asked me if I wanted a check then or if I would send him an assessment. I told him an assessment would take a couple of months, and he would owe interest on the sum.

"If you want to save the interest," I said, "give me a check right now."

He wrote the check and I returned to Charlotte with it in hand. I was making $250 a month, and here I was bringing in three years' salary on the first audit I did.

Ruth and I were just getting by on my salary. I was doing so much traveling I wanted to get an Esso credit card. Esso had revoked my card while we were in San Francisco. When I tried to get another one they wouldn't answer my letters. Finally, I went by the Esso offices in Charlotte in person.

"Mr. Ketner, you don't make enough money to qualify for an Esso credit card," a gentleman told me after looking over my records.

"I'm glad to hear that," I told him. "Tell me again, how do you spell your name? I want to be sure I get your name correct because I'm with the State Revenue Department. I don't know whether you noticed that or not. I want to make sure when I write my boss and tell him that you said I was a credit risk because the State Revenue Department doesn't pay enough."

"Just one minute, Mr. Ketner," he said. He came back in a couple of minutes with my credit card.

Two things happened that convinced me to leave the Revenue Department. One was during an audit of a little service station. I was with an experienced auditor, and he asked the owner how many cases of Coca-Colas he sold a week. The guy didn't answer.

"Would you say you sell 10 cases a week," my boss asked.

"Yeah," the guy agreed.

I looked over and saw just three cases of empties in the whole place. I asked the service station operator how often the Coca-Cola man came, and he said once a week. The guy didn't sell but a case or two of drinks a week, so I told the auditor that the 10-case figure was an error.

The boss didn't care.

"We try to raise so much money at each stop," he said.

"This job's not for me," I told him.

The other thing that convinced me to leave the Revenue Department was Ruth. She was pregnant. I figured it was time for me to settle down. I called Glenn and told him I was ready if he needed somebody at Excel.

"Let me talk to you and Ruth," he said. "I want to make sure you know the rules."

The rules were: Glenn made the rules, and I followed them. He said that I would be expected to devote myself, 100 percent, to the job, make it the most important thing in my life. If there was something at work that needed doing, I would be expected to cancel any other plans without hesitation. I assured my brother that it was time for me to settle down and start a real career.

Glenn remains the smartest man I've ever met.

I think Glenn was trying to teach me a lesson the first few months I worked for him. He had me taking inventory at a store every Monday morning by myself. Nobody can do it by himself — but I did it. I'd leave at 4 or 5 o'clock in the morning and get there and take inventory. It would take 14, 15 hours. He had a company car that didn't have a heater or an air-conditioner in it. He didn't want anyone being comfortable. You'd get there faster. After six or eight weeks, I began teaming up with Brown, Bill Smith and Jim Berrier to do inventories. The four of us would travel together every Monday morning, regular as clockwork, to take inventory. Glenn didn't believe in expense accounts, so we would guess the time we would finish the inventory with the loser buying breakfast. The four of us, the store manager and another employee would put our guesses in an envelope before we started. We didn't open the envelope until after breakfast. Boy, that got hairy, because we weren't making any money to start with. You could tell the ones who thought they had won. They ordered ham and eggs. But the ones with a bad guess would order a sweet roll or something cheap.

Inventory was taken at retail, meaning the quantity on hand was counted and called to the writer (me) along with the selling price, i.e. 48 at 39. The inventory form had one column for each figure, 1-50, and entering the quantities was easy when you started. But as the form (roughly 24 inches by 14) filled, it was harder for the eye to follow the correct column as numbers were only at the top. There were only two forms available. National

Cash Register Co. had the better of the two, and it was poorly done.

After years of complaining about the forms available I drew up my own form and called it "Sur-Chex." I got the form copyrighted, and started selling them all over the United States, but calculators came along and ended that idea. In hindsight, I should have "lit a candle rather than curse the darkness." I would have made a lot of money.

I was Glenn's buyer, bookkeeper, accounts payable clerk, inventory control man. I did everything. When a shipment would come in for Excel Grocery, the warehouse man Howard Kennedy would come in and say, "We just got another 100 cases, and I don't know where it's going." The warehouse was that tight. And Ketner's stores' books would never balance, so I would go and balance their books. I saw an ad in the paper one day for George S. Mays Company of Chicago. It was a consulting company that would streamline your office for $100. I figured I would pay the $100 if Glenn wouldn't, so I wouldn't have to do all that straightening out for Ketner's.

The Mays guy came down and said, "This is the first time we've ever gone to a company that's making money like it's going out of style."

"I didn't call you because we're having trouble making money," I said. "I just wanted you to help get the office straightened out. But I have designed a form that has eliminated 99 percent of our problem, so I don't really need you at all."

The consultant talked to Glenn and told him he had the best-run operation he had ever seen, but he saw some areas where he could improve. For $20 an hour, he would study his operation and make some suggestions. Keep in mind that I was making $35 a week, so I watched this guy pretty closely. He was good. Glenn had eight stores then. He analyzed every expense item in every store — laundry, supplies, and so forth — and recorded the best one. He then took the lowest expense cost for each item of the entire chain and told Glenn that he should use this figure as the average from then on. Simple, but it worked.

One day I walked in and he was drinking a Coca-Cola.

"What are you doing?" I bellowed. "Man, you're making $20 an hour. That's 33 and a third cents a minute. It takes you five minutes to drink a Coca-Cola, that's a dollar sixty-six and two-thirds cents to drink a nickel Coca-Cola. Not around here you don't. If you've been going to the toilet on my time, we won't go along with that. From here on, you go to the toilet before you come and after you leave. I don't want to see you smoking a cigarette because at 33 and a third cents a minute, I can't afford to have you smoking."

"If I come in 15 minutes early and leave 15 minutes late, can I live a normal life?" he asked.

"If you do that," I said, "it'll be OK." He agreed.

Glenn owned a little service station right beside his grocery store at Innes and Lee streets. Zeke Gamble ran it for him, and I inventoried it every Saturday night.

One day Glenn called and said, "You've got to go up there. Zeke's resigned, and I can't talk him out of it."

I went to the service station and asked Zeke why he was quitting. He said somebody else had offered him $250 a month, and Glenn was paying him only $60 a week.

"Zeke, $60 a week is more than $250 a month," I said. "There are four and a third weeks in a month."

Zeke didn't look like he understood.

"Do you buy there are 52 weeks in a year? Sixty times 52 is $3,120. That's $260 a month. Now you want to go to work for somebody for $250 a month? Twelve times $250 is what, $3,000. You're being taken for $120."

Glenn had used all the logic in the world on him, but he hadn't gotten down to the nitty-gritty of the problem. Zeke didn't know there were four and a third weeks in a month.

Ruth and I attended First Presbyterian Church of Salisbury, and I served as chairman of the associate board, which was responsible for ushering and taking up collections. One Sunday, the congregation was to vote on the rotation of Elders. Up until then, Elders were elected for life. Some members of First Church were attempting to change to the rotation system, but the Elders in charge, obviously, did not want to give up their positions and opposed the change. They did agree to have a congregational meeting and let the members of the church vote.

The meeting started shortly after the sermon ended at noon, and it soon became obvious that the Elders in charge intended to filibuster until most of the congregation had left. Their supporters were prepared to stay all day, if necessary. People began to leave within 20 minutes.

As chairman of the ushers, I was responsible for passing out the ballots. Acting on my own, I stationed ushers at the doors and let people vote as they left. After another 15 minutes of the filibuster, the Elders saw that their ploy had failed, and they permitted the minister to call for the vote. I asked the son of the ringleader to help count the ballots so there could be no question as to whether the results were falsified. I had a feeling the old guard was going to be defeated, because as people left the meeting they asked which way to vote to be sure they were voting against those doing the filibuster.

I called the minister immediately after the meeting and gave him the results. I apologized if my actions had been wrong. I explained that I thought the purpose of the meeting was to vote. The matter went before the Presbytery to decide whether my actions were in order. The Presbytery decided that I was correct and ordered that the rotation system be implemented at First Church in Salisbury. The change proved to be extremely important to the growth of the church.

One of the most valuable things I learned while working with Glenn was how to negotiate with food brokers and big companies. I learned to sell myself to the seller. Jerry Frye was one of those who routinely called on Excel Grocery. He represented 20 to 30 accounts. On this particular day, Neville Majors, president of Old Virginia Packing Company, came with him. He had a deal on strawberry preserves: $4.74 for a case of 12 or 39 1/2 cents each.

I said, "Jerry, I'll take 1,000 cases and ship them all out to the stores. We'll sell them for 39 cents, break even, won't make a penny, but I'll distribute them for you if you'll sell them to me for $4.68."

The president spoke up: "No, Mr. Ketner, I won't take your deal."

I looked over and said, "Jerry, would you mind introducing this gentleman. I got confused when you introduced me."

And he said, "It's Mr. Majors."

I came back, "I got his name all right. His title got me messed up."

Mr. Majors said, "I'm president."

I said, "Jerry, I'll take 1,000 cases for $4.68."

Mr. Majors said, "No, Mr. Ketner."

I said, "Jerry, you didn't tell me he married the boss's daughter."

Mr. Majors said, "I didn't marry the boss's daughter."

I said, "Jerry, I'll take 1,000 cases at $4.68."

Mr. Majors said, "No, Mr. Ketner."

I said, "Well, Jerry, you didn't tell me that he inherited the company and that's how he got to be president."

Mr. Majors said, "No, I didn't inherit the damn company."

And I said, "Well, I'll take 1,000 cases at $4.68."

Mr. Majors said, "Mr. Ketner, I don't know what's wrong with you, but you just can't understand I'm not taking it."

I said, "I am kind of confused. We established you're the president. We established you didn't marry the boss's daughter. We established you didn't inherit the company."

Mr. Majors said, "That's right."

I said, "With those three known factors, I've got a right, I think, to assume I'm talking to an intelligent person."

Mr. Majors said, "Well, I'd like to hope you are."

I said, "Well, I would, too. But you tell me what intelligent person turns down a 1,000-case order. We're only six cents a case apart. That's $60. With Uncle Sam's 50 percent tax bracket, that's $30 they want to pay. That leaves $30. Now the State of Virginia says, 'Let me have 7 percent.' That's $2.10. So we're $27.90 apart on 1,000 cases, packed 12 to a case. I'm going to move 12,000 units for you for $27.90. Now you tell me what intelligent person would turn down your order?"

Mr. Majors said, "Jerry, write up the damn order."

A buyer has to be a better salesman. I've got to convince him that what I want is in his best interest. So many people get hung up on percentages. You can't take percentages to the bank. If you want proof, take a deposit slip and write 25% on it. They'd give it back to you. Make it 50%, they'd give it back. But you put $5, they will keep it. So you take dollars to the bank and that became my philosophy. I'd rather make *five fast pennies than one slow nickel*. It separates the men from the boys. We'd rather sell *five cans* of beans at 1 cents profit each, making a nickel, where our competitors would rather make a nickel on *one can*.

I also found out that you had to fight just as hard to keep what was rightfully yours in dealing with grocery manufacturers. If an invoice was for $1,000 and the delivery was $100 short, I'd still take $20 discount, even though 2 percent of $1,000 is $20 and 2 percent of $900 is $18. The logic was that if it came later, I wouldn't have to recalculate my discount. That happened on a Proctor and Gamble order once and they called from Cincinnati to say I had taken too much discount on an order that was $90 short.

"If you hadn't shorted me that $90, I would have made 10 percent on the merchandise," I told him. "You owe me $9 more.

How could I have overlooked that? I'm getting careless." The guy said to forget that he had called and hung up.

All manufacturers will occasionally run a discount price on a shipment: 25 cents off a box of detergent, instant coffee, and the like. To prevent the retail grocer from losing money, the companies would reduce their price. Items that carried a 25-cent discount on their labels and were packed 12 to a case were reduced $3 to the grocer.

That was fine — as far as it went. But the first time I looked at an invoice for a carload of a discounted product from, say, Proctor and Gamble, it struck me that while the retail customer was getting a price break on the merchandise, Excel Grocery Company deserved a discount — and wasn't getting one.

A carload of the detergent Tide, for example, might cost $10,000 if the product carried no cents-off label. The standard 2 percent discount for paying the bill within 10 days lowered the cost $200. A carload of Tide with a cents-off label cost $9,000, and the 2 percent discount was $180. Excel Grocery didn't make one extra dime selling this load of Tide, and I felt we should get the full discount: $200. If Proctor and Gamble wanted to give my customers 25 cents, that was their business. They weren't going to penalize me $20 in the process.

On the next carload of specially priced merchandise we received from Proctor and Gamble, I took a discount on the gross amount. I got a patronizing letter from the accounting department explaining that the allowable discount was only $180. It appeared to me that they didn't believe I knew how to figure a simple percentage and were giving me lessons. I wrote them back, stating my opinion. They disagreed with it and eventually won their case because Proctor and Gamble was bigger than Excel Grocery Company.

While I lost that battle, I had not given up on the war. An identical situation came up with Nestle Company over a carload of Nescafe Instant Coffee with 25 cents off each jar. I used the same strategy as I had with Proctor and Gamble, deducting my discount on the gross amount.

Nestle informed me that I was entitled to a discount on the net amount and that I owed them $20. I wrote them back, sticking to my guns. Each time Nestle replied, the letter came from a higher department. This went on for months and while Nestle wasn't giving in, I could see that they were taking me seriously.

Finally a letter came from a vice president. "Mr. Ketner, the 2 percent discount is for use of the money. You only had the use of $9,000 so therefore two percent is $180."

I wrote back, "You're wrong. The 2 percent is not for use of the money. It's a custom you got in the habit of giving. You don't need money so badly that you pay 2 percent for 10 days. That's 73 percent a year. If you need money that badly, I figure that I should get a brokerage fee if I can find it cheaper. So I went to Wachovia Bank and Trust Co. and found that you have a triple A credit rating. Wachovia is willing to lend you $5 million at 6 percent. Now I'm saving you 67 percent on $5 million, so I'm certainly entitled to something for that. Please credit my account $20."

I got a beautiful letter back. The letter, I thought, agreed with me, oh, gosh, in big words. I had no idea what they meant, but it got to the last and it said, "Mr. Ketner, unless you send us the $20, we will never send you any more merchandise." I looked up some of the big words in the dictionary, and found that I had never been called stupid in such nice ways.

I wrote Nestle back that it was going to win this argument, not because it was right but because it was bigger and we couldn't do without its products. I paid under protest and wrote all over the check "Paid under protest."

Three months later we bought another shipment. Nescafe again had a 25 cents off label, but the invoice said, "Take cash discount on gross amount." I'd won. I wrote the vice president: "I know this is going to come as a shock to you that someone with my limited intelligence is still in business. An even bigger shock to you is that we still have the same post office box, which means we have been able to pay the rent. What I'm saying in a nice way is since I paid you under protest, please send back my $20."

I didn't get a letter from them. I got a phone call. "Mr. Ketner," the vice president said, "we've been up here waiting on your letter. You didn't let us down."

"That's really good," I said, "but how about my $20?"

"Let me tell you what happened," the vice president said. "I took your folder, which is about a half-inch thick into a board meeting, just for laughs. Everyone died laughing, except the president. 'Read me those figures again,' he said. 'He's right. We are taking $20 away from the buyer."

"That's good," I said, "but how about my $20?"

"That's what I told the president you would say," the vice president said, "and he asked if you would take a moral victory instead of a financial one."

"Could you tell me what bank to deposit it in and what percent they will give me?" I asked.

Anyway, they were the first to break down. Now everybody in the country gives cash discount on gross amount. It's deserved. It's legitimate. And nobody, except me, knows why they are getting it.

I enjoyed fighting with the big boys, even over a dollar. Kraft had a promotion that promised a silver dollar to anyone sending in three labels from salad dressing jars. Ruth and I were watching every penny in our personal budget, so I bought three of the 35-cent jars and attempted to take off the labels. It was impossible. I soaked the jars. Still no luck. Finally, I wrote the president of Kraft and told him that if he would tell me how to get the labels off, I would send him a silver dollar. Kraft wrote back, saying they too were unable to remove the labels. The letter contained a silver dollar. I'm sure I was one of the few people in the United States to collect on this promotion that failed so miserably. Perhaps I'm wrong in saying the promotion failed. Many people may have bought salad dressing intending to collect the silver dollar before finding it impossible.

The one fight I never won was over soft drink bottle deposits. The bottlers only charge it in the Southeast. Apparently, they think everybody in the South is stupid. And they get by with it in the 10 states in the Southeast.

You buy a Coke. I charge you a dime for the bottle. You bring it back. I give you a dime. Then I give it to Coke, and they give me a dime. I've handled that bottle 11 times, swapping money. The bottlers are smart, and I admire smart people. They don't bill you for the contents and the bottles together. They have separate invoices. Back in the old days, Coca-Cola charged $2.40 a case, and the bottles cost a nickel, which was $1.20. So they would bill you for 50 cases of drinks and 50 cases of bottles. You would get credit for the bottles you returned. That would keep you from realizing you're not getting any markup on the bottles. If they billed you just once, you could see the cost was $3.60 and you would base your markup accordingly.

I never picked that up for Excel Grocery or Ketner's, but years later for Food Lion I wrote all the companies trying to get them to combine the billing so we would get markup on the whole thing or charge us 8 cents for a bottle and let us make 2 cents for handling it. I talked to Frank Outlaw with Bi-Lo, and he kicked every returnable bottle out of his stores. I didn't have the guts to do that, but I asked A&P, Kroger and Winn-Dixie to join in the protest. Nobody would do it. And I think the reason is that nobody wanted to admit how stupid they had been — and, yes, still are.

In 1955, Ketner's had 10 stores and ambition to grow. Glenn merged his operation with John Milner's Piggly-Wiggly chain of 15 stores headquartered in Raleigh. Glenn owned 51 percent of the stock, so what he said went.

The merger was exciting, and everyone in the Ketner operation thought we were really going places. Glenn had become one of the Southeast's larger independent grocers. The merger brought me into contact with Hugh Simons, of Milner's Piggly Wiggly. We were talking and I found that they had also used the services of the George S. Mays Company, but with unsatisfactory results. They didn't like the Mays consultant, so none of his recommendations were implemented. That sounded foolish to me, and I told Hugh that it was like going to the doctor and then not following his advice about how to get well.

Another area of the merger involved the two warehouses. Hugh and I worked on combining inventories in Salisbury and Raleigh. In 95 percent of the cases, both companies carried identical merchandise, but once in a while we would come across a fast-moving item that Ketner's carried but Piggly Wiggly didn't. I would ask Hugh why he hadn't stocked such popular items, and he explained that the salesman had made him or Mr. Milner mad.

"That's not going to happen any more," I said. "If you want to get mad at a salesman, then do it at home. Your job now is to run your area of operation for the customers' benefit."

The Ketner-Piggly Wiggly chain seemed poised to dominate the grocery business in North Carolina. Its 25 stores stretched along the new Interstate 85 from Salisbury to Raleigh with plenty of opportunities to expand.

I should have known something was up because Glenn took Jim Berrier and me to a meeting in Miami and didn't say one word about the cost of the meals we ordered. We didn't know he was getting ready to sell his operation to Winn-Dixie. It turned out that he was.

Glenn called a meeting of all his employees at the Yadkin Hotel to make the announcement. Tears flowed in buckets that night. A lot of people were upset. I looked at Winn-Dixie as another opportunity. If I was good enough to do the job then everything would be great. If not, I didn't want to worry about that.

Glenn signed a non-competitive agreement with Winn-Dixie and about two weeks after the sale, he asked me to sign something. It was an agreement not to go back in business.

"I've never been in business," I said. "How can I not go back in business?"

"You know what I'm talking about," Glenn said.

"Well," I said, "how much are you going to pay me?"

"Nothing," he said.

"Well, I'm not going to sign anything I don't get paid for." I said. "You've received several million dollars, or whatever you got."

"Well," he said, "I'm not going to pay you anything."

Glenn went to Brown, too. And Brown wanted to know if I had signed it.

"Well, I won't sign anything that Ralph won't sign," he said. "If he had signed it, I still might not sign."

If he had offered us $500, I would have signed the agreement so fast it would have made your head spin. But, thank goodness, he didn't.

Winn-Dixie led some of us to believe it was going to build a big warehouse in Salisbury, but Raleigh was the first choice all along. It was my job to stock it, and Wertz Nease, division manager, asked me how much money I was going to need from Jacksonville, Winn-Dixie's headquarters.

I told him I could let them have a million or two dollars.

"What are you talking about?" he asked.

"When I place the original order, I'm going to ask for the usual 45-day dating," I said.

"I've never heard of that," Mr. Nease said.

"I haven't either," I said, "but I'm going to write a two-page letter with every order and the first page and nine-tenths of the second page are going to be just nothing. I hope they won't read the last paragraph. It's going to ask for the usual 45-day dating and say, 'If I don't hear otherwise, I know this meets your approval.' They're not going to read two pages and we'll get the 45 days to pay automatically. We're entitled to it."

If you have just one warehouse and you build another, you've got to stock everything in the new warehouse and continue to stock everything in the old warehouse. So you've got duplicate inventory for the benefit of the suppliers. It's legitimate. Nobody ever thought about it until I did. Now everybody gets it. I changed the whole industry.

I was very happy working for Winn-Dixie. They gave me an option to buy stock on credit and deducted the cost from my paycheck on a monthly basis. I was head buyer, the No. 2 man in North Carolina. Things seemed to be working out pretty well. But my brother, Brown, hated it. And the Winn-Dixie people weren't wild about him either.

Brown was a meat buyer, and I was the grocery man. Saturday mornings we would meet with the corporate people to discuss the items we were going to feature next week. Brown told them what he thought. He planned to sell whole chickens for 25 cents a pound and cut-up chickens for 29 cents a pound.

"Brown, you know you can't charge more for cut-up chickens than you do for whole chickens," said Mr. Nease, division manager.

Nobody did then. It was asinine that they didn't, but nobody did. It was unheard of.

"You're right Mr. Nease," Brown said. "You can never charge more for cut-up chickens."

So it came back around and everybody restated their specials. Brown said: "Whole chickens 25 cents, cut-up chickens 29 cents.

"Brown," Mr. Nease said, "I thought we had that clarified. You cannot charge more for cut-up chickens."

"I agree with you," Brown said. "Nobody should ever do that. I just charge less for whole ones."

They didn't think Brown was funny, but I nearly busted a gut trying not to laugh.

By the next year, Brown, Wilson Smith and I were ready to take the biggest gamble we'd ever taken. We planned to quit Winn-Dixie, go back to Salisbury and open our own store. It would be called Food Town.

Food Town Founders

Ralph W. Ketner, *President*

Brown Ketner, *Vice President*   Wilson Smith, *Secretary*

Pictures Courtesy of Salisbury Post

5. Buddy, Can You Spare $1,000?

Wilson Smith picked up the telephone book in the old Excel Grocery warehouse and started calling out names. Wilson, my brother, Brown, and I had decided to start a new grocery store in Salisbury, but we had one problem. We had no money.

We decided to ask everyone we knew to invest in our store by buying stock at $10 a share.

We had scraped together $62,500 on our own, but that was only about half of what we needed to stock the big new store my older brother, Glenn, was building in Ketner Center on the western edge of town.

The three of us had quit good jobs with Winn-Dixie in 1957. When Glenn sold Ketner-Milner's in 1956, we were part of the deal, and the three of us learned how Winn-Dixie operated from the inside. Winn-Dixie even gave me a stock option and let me pay monthly. Well, the stock went up tremendously in the year I worked for them, and when I told them I wanted to start my own store in Salisbury, they didn't want to let me exercise the option. I had to threaten to sue to get the stock, and I sold it to raise a good part of the money I put up for Food Town.

I'm sure that didn't sit too well with the Winn-Dixie people. And they probably didn't like the idea that Glenn was leasing us his building either. He had agreed not to go back into the grocery business, and he didn't. But he could build and lease a grocery store — besides Winn-Dixie had already turned him down on this new location on West Innes Street.

We were hoping that people around Salisbury would be a little confused about Glenn's role in our new store. They'd be a lot more inclined to invest if they thought the "smart Ketner" was behind it, and we didn't go to any great lengths to explain the situation unless they asked a lot of questions.

We took that telephone book and found only 250 names of people we thought might invest: Paul Ritchie at the post office and Charlie Barger at The Salisbury Post, Jake and Zeda Barger of Faith, Ken Brown at Salisbury Engravers and the Hurleys at the newspaper. J. F. Hurley, Sr. said he bought it because he knew he had an advertising customer. He gave the stock, 100 shares each, to his sons, because he didn't want it to look like The Post favored one grocery store over another. Most of the people we called were not well-informed or well educated about the stock market. They were our friends. They believed in us.

One person made millions of dollars on Food Town by mistake. Julian Robertson got a call from Smith, but he thought it was his neighbor Bill Smith, president of Security Bank, calling about a new offering. Robertson asked if Smith was going to buy any, and naturally Smith said he was putting all he could in the new stock. "That's good enough for me, Robertson said. "Put me down for $2,000 worth."

There were small investors, too. Seven or eight people bought just five shares, $50 worth. Those five shares today would be 97,200 shares as the original stock has split 19,440 for 1.

When we officially went public in 1970, we found that we had technically violated the law by calling 250 people to invest in the company. The underwriter taking us public explained that if we had over 10 shareholders, it was necessary to register with the SEC. My answer then was that "We weren't in the Southeastern Conference. What did I care about the SEC?"

I enjoy telling people that we succeeded because of ignorance. In our first six months of operation we were literally bankrupt, but we had no attorney to tell us. I went on the assumption that unless you had zero money, you weren't broke. I didn't know we were bankrupt, so I kept working. I didn't know we couldn't call people on the telephone, so we did.

It reminds me of the football team that was undefeated, but found itself four points behind in the last game of the season with time for just four plays. The coach sent in the first play, and the quarterback was smeared. He sent in the second play, and the quarterback was again smeared, and on the third play, the quarterback was smeared. So the coach, not wanting to take full blame for losing the game, told the quarterback to call the fourth play himself. He did, and the team scored a touchdown and won the game.

In the locker room, the coach said to the quarterback, "That was great. You saved our undefeated season, but wasn't that Play 15 you called?

"Yes," the quarterback said.

"We haven't used Play 15 all year because it has never worked, even in practice. How did you dream of using it?

"Coach," the quarterback said, "it was simple. It was fourth down and nine to go. Four and nine are fifteen.

"Four and nine are thirteen, not fifteen," the coach said.

"The quarterback counted his fingers and looked up at the coach. "If I were as smart as you Coach, we would have lost that ball game."

Winn-Dixie had two stores in Salisbury and was waiting to throw the book at us as soon as we opened. Brown said he heard that Winn-Dixie had set aside $2 million to bankrupt us.

"That's when I knew we were going to make it," he said years later. "They could have given us $1 million, and we never would have opened that store. They couldn't be too smart."

Food Lion erected a marker outside its store No. 1
at Ketner Center in 1990.

Food Town No. 1 at Ketner Center in Salisbury. "It's big," an
advertisement in 1957 began. "It's beautiful. It's bountiful. Salisbury's
newest, largest and most modern food store. More than 100 years
experience behind the management of Food Town Stores." *Photo
courtesy of The Salisbury Post.*

But Winn-Dixie was determined to try to put us out of business. They matched all our weekend specials and brought in truckloads of merchandise. We sold Coca-Colas for a nickel a carton, bread for a nickel a loaf. Salisbury was written up in "Supermarket News" as one of the five most competitive areas in the United States. I felt sorry for the other four, because we were going broke in a hurry.

When we opened, the parking lot wasn't paved. And we operated for months with a gravel lot. That hurt business, and if it hadn't been for those original stockholders and the Catawba College students and professors shopping with us, we wouldn't have made it. Six months went by, and we lost half of our original investment. We weren't smart enough to know we were bankrupt.

Clifford Ray, one of our produce men, along with Tommy Eller, opened a vegetable stand on East Innes Street that first year. There were days he made more money than we did, and he kept us afloat. We did anything to survive.

Brown thought that no one should ever beat us on price. We were fighting Winn-Dixie, which had millions of dollars backing it. All they had to do was fight us for six months, or even six weeks, and we would go under if we were foolish enough to meet their prices.

After six months, I told Brown that since I was president, I wanted to be the one to lose the other half of our investment. So I started tying our specials to a $10 or $15 food order. That was the first time that had been done. Now everybody, except Food Lion, does it.

We turned it around in the second half of that year and opened a second store at East Innes and Long streets the next year. Winn-Dixie stopped trying to bankrupt us. I guess they figured that if they couldn't put us out of business with one store they weren't going to do it with two.

Business was fun, even though it was a struggle. I enjoyed everything, even an occasional round with my brother, Glenn. He built us a little office beside the store in Ketner Center. And I went in the bathroom for the first time and saw there was no mirror or toilet paper holder. I called Glenn and told him the contractor forgot to put a toilet paper holder and a mirror in there.

"No," he said, "the contract doesn't call for it."

"I'll make it easy on you," I said. "I won't pay you any rent until you get a toilet paper holder and a mirror in that bathroom. We both have the same lawyer. I can't afford to pay him, so you better call him if you want to get an expert's advice on whether you have to put up a toilet paper holder and a mirror."

Glenn called back in 30 minutes and said, "I'll buy it, but I won't put it up."

"If it requires me to tighten one screw," I said, "the answer is not no, it's hell no. It's either up and in good shape, or I'm not paying rent."

About an hour or two later, he came out himself and put them up. He left the price tags on: 19 cents on the little metal toilet paper holder and 39 cents on the mirror.

He's hard, I tell you.

My brother, Brown, on the other hand, was a laugh a minute. I remember a woman who came into the store with her little boy. He moved the plastic shelf tags as he walked down the aisles. She kept saying, "Johnny, don't do that." But he kept right on. Finally, Brown whispered something in his ear, and he didn't touch another tag. When they checked out, the woman asked Brown what he had told the child to make him behave. "I told him that if he touched another one of those tags I was going to knock his teeth out," Brown said.

I call the first 10 years we were in business "R & D — research and development, a fancy way of saying we were starving to death. We tried every kind of gimmick to get people to shop with us. We were a "me too" grocery store, offering the same things as our competition: weekly specials, trading stamps, contests. We didn't do anything to earn a customer's business. One unusual idea I had was to sell Food Town customers gasoline at absolute cost. Our only expense would be the person who pumped the gas. He wouldn't check oil or tires or wipe your windshield or anything. There was an empty station a few blocks from our store at Ketner Center, so I called the owner, Sink Walser, with a proposition.

"Sink, I'd like to lease your service station. The only thing is that I don't want to pay you any rent."

"What do you mean?" he asked.

"I'm not going to pay you a penny rent."

"I'm not going to let you do that."

"How much are you getting for it now? You're getting nothing. I'm offering nothing. You're no worse off. You make your money as a distributor. If I distribute this gasoline for you, then you're making money on every gallon I pump."

Then I explained what I planned to do. He said it sounded like a good idea. We opened the station and overnight became the No. 1 station in Salisbury. Every customer had to have a $15 cash register tape from Food Town. If you didn't have that, you couldn't buy gas. We wouldn't sell it to you at any price because the pumps were at absolute cost, 10 to 15 cents a gallon lower than the other service stations in town.

We were pumping so much gas that Brown and Bill talked me into adding another employee and trying to sell motor oil, wash the windshield — become a full service station. So instead of one man handling the business, it took three, and it cost too much. We just gave up on the whole deal. But it was an excellent idea, I thought. Today it would work even better because people are used to pumping their own gas.

One Saturday morning, while working in the office, I got a call from a lady. "Mr. Ketner, do you know that there is no toilet paper in the Capitol Theater?"

"I beg your pardon," I said.

"There's no toilet paper in the bathroom of the Capitol Theater," she repeated.

"Lady, I have lots of problems, but thank goodness. . ." then I stopped. "You are calling because Food Town is sponsoring the Saturday morning kids' movie, aren't you? Which restroom is it that has no toilet paper?"

She said it was the ladies' room. I asked her to check the men's room, too. It was empty. I called Paul Phillips, owner of the theater, and told him about the situation.

"Ralph," he said, "there's never any toilet paper in the restrooms during a kids' movie. They take it out and throw it all over the theater. Tell that woman to stick some paper in her child's pocket next time they come to the movies."

I could see his point, too. The problems you run into if you try to do anything out of the ordinary.

Nothing stopped me from trying. I had another idea: prescriptions at cost. I was in Charlotte one day at a drugstore picking up something and I saw a person give the prescription to a pharmacist. "That'll be $16," the pharmacist said before filling it. Maybe I was wrong, but I could see this man calculating two days work or whatever to get this $16 back as opposed to seeing his children get well. Finally, he said. "Well, I've got to have it."

My thought was that if I could come up with some way to sell prescriptions at cost to everybody it would be a service to mankind and at the same time it would probably increase sales for us.

It was years later that I tried the idea. Mark Drugs in Salisbury put an ad in the paper that it was going out of business, so I went and talked to Mark. I said I'd had this idea for several years and since he was going out of business, why not try it?

"Why don't you delay it for a few months," I said. "I'll pay you $50 a week if you fill all prescriptions for customers with a card from us showing that they're entitled to a prescription at cost. You'll make your money off sales at the front end."

I told Mark I wasn't worried about his cheating on the idea because his competition was going to make sure he was selling at cost. They would send people in to check. Nobody ever accused him of cheating.

Mark agreed to try it, and his prescription volume went up over 300 percent in one week just because we sent our customers to him. But we couldn't work out the deal in Lexington or Kannapolis — we had stores in those towns — and so we couldn't advertise it. The only place I could tell people about it was in Salisbury. People loved it. But after eight or 10 weeks, I got tired of paying him the $50 because our sales didn't go up. I tried to cut it to $25 a week, but he wouldn't do it. So we just quit that one, too. Mark stayed in business another 10 to 15 years on the new business he generated. I would love to get back to that idea. I've even got the trade name: PAC — Prescriptions At Cost.

Goodwill makes good business, and I believe Food Town made a lot of friends in its early years by sending a bud vase to people in the hospital in Salisbury. Bob Jones, owner of J & M Florist in Salisbury, and I worked out the idea. I told him he would get almost as much benefit from the promotion as Food Town because J & M Florist's name would be on the card sent with every bud vase. For over 10 years, we sent more than 10 bud vases a day to new patients at Rowan Memorial Hospital and we included every new mother. The Gray Ladies, hospital volunteers, tried to give our bud vases to those patients who received no flowers and we received a tremendous number of calls from the recipients. Bob and I estimated that we gave away more than $100,000 in flowers. I'm sure many of those people became Food Town shoppers.

When I wasn't trying to increase sales, I had to find ways to cut costs. During our early years, we burned cardboard and had tremendous problems with the Environmental Protection Agency because of smoke emissions. It was costing us literally, millions of dollars to burn cardboard, and it was an easy decision to start bailing it for recycling. We made millions instead. Now, Food Lion is being sued by the government claiming child labor law violations over the recycling of cardboard. The law in 1961 was that 16- and 17-year-olds could put cardboard and other trash in the bailer without being in violation, In 1992, someone reading the law decided that, in effect, a new product had been "manufactured" in the process. Under these conditions, someone in Washington decided that those people 16 and 17 years old had technically violated the law by throwing cardboard and trash into a non-operating bailer. For 31 years, this had not been the law. Then someone came up with a new interpretation, subjecting Food Lion and other supermarkets and bailer users throughout the country to possible violations and suits. It is idiotic, and if the government continues such ridiculous interpretations of laws passed by Congress, it can only result in retailers being forced to discontinue using anyone under 18 years of age as an employee.

I have often said, if you go by the book, you're going to starve to death. Everybody has read the book. You've got to write the book. To me, that was writing the book, trying all of these different things.

Kraft Foods had a promotion on candy that would give $20,000 to equip a Little League field to the team that turned in the most candy wrappers. Boy, my mind immediately started to click. OK, one team in Salisbury would enter the contest. I was going to tie it in with the Boy Scouts, Little League, school system. Everybody would work together for that one team. I wanted to get the support of our county and city school superintendents, the YMCA, Scouts, Little League teams and Jaycees. I invited these leaders to a T-bone steak dinner where I explained what I thought would guarantee Salisbury winning this $20,000.

If one kid would sell one bag of candy per month in the school during this promotion, and if the Boy Scouts could do so and so, the absolute minimum we would turn in would be 200,000 wrappers. Kraft's requirement was that everybody had to buy the candy at retail, but I agreed to rebate every penny profit to the schools. They thought it was a wonderful idea, but nobody wanted to head up the drive. The Jaycees backed out; everybody backed out. So we just didn't do it.

Months later, I asked the Kraft man who won. He found out the winner turned in 200 or 300 bags. We would have done that much in 10 minutes.

Later the Jaycees came to me about helping underwrite a Little League field. "Where were you," I asked, "when I offered to hand you $20,000 and you wouldn't do any work to help me?"

I had another idea that didn't work out exactly as planned when I bought all the tickets to Salisbury's Class D professional baseball team for one evening and gave them to Food Town customers for each grocery order of $10 or more. Average attendance at the games was 200 to 300, but this night there were 3,000 people at the park for the ball game. Suddenly, I realized that I had forgotten about the concession stand. If the regular concessionaires charged high prices, people might think we were trying to trick them. I bought the concession stand to avoid any criticism, and we sold hot dogs and drinks at a nickel each. That cost three times more than all the tickets to the game.

There were problems at every turn. My Uncle Charlie, my father's brother, was the market manager for us in Kannapolis. He called one day and said his health insurance had been cancelled. Mutual of Omaha had studied his application form from 19 years earlier and found he had left one item blank. Under the law, this allowed the company to cancel Uncle Charlie's insurance.

Charlie asked me for help. I wrote Mutual of Omaha. The company was within its rights, a letter explained. I wrote the North Carolina Commissioner of Insurance twice and only receive form letters explaining the company was within its rights. Finally, I called Clyde Harriss, the Rowan County representative to the N.C. General Assembly. I asked him to personally tell the commissioner of insurance that unless he did something about Uncle Charlie's problem, I would take out a full page ad in the newspaper asking people not to vote for him.

It got results. The insurance commissioner came to see me and said that what Mutual of Omaha was doing was not right. He showed me a copy of a letter he had prepared, telling Mutual of Omaha that its right to do business in North Carolina was to be canceled unless the problem with Uncle Charlie was handled to a satisfactory conclusion. Two days later, Mutual of Omaha called to explain that it had reconsidered Uncle Clarlie's claim and would honor it. It's a shame you have to take such action to get results.

Another case involved problems we were having with our National Cash Register machines. The service department in Charlotte just couldn't seem to correct the problems, so I wrote the president of National Cash Register Co. in Dayton, Ohio.

Dear Sir:

Allow me to introduce myself. I am Ralph W. Ketner, president and treasurer of Food Town Stores, Inc. We have five Food Town Stores.

Each store has five NCR cash registers.

The next two years we hope to open five more stores.

Each of these stores will be equipped with someone's cash register.

Now that I, hopefully, have your attention, let me tell you my problem. My problem is that your service representatives have done such a poor job that we will probably not continue to do business with NCR unless the problem is corrected.

Yours very truly,
Ralph W. Ketner

I sent a carbon copy of the letter to the service department in Charlotte. About two weeks later the service department called and asked what the president had to say.

"You have a problem there," I said. "Either your president can't read or write, as I haven't received a reply from him."

Within 30 minutes, I got a telephone call from a fellow saying he was a vice president with National Cash Register in Dayton, Ohio. He wanted to talk to be about my problem with NCR.

"I don't know what you are talking about," I said. "I don't know of any problem."

"Didn't you write the president regarding a problem?" he asked.

"Yes, I do have a problem with the president but not with the vice president. I did not write you. My problem concerns the president of NCR, and unless he can't read or write, I do not want to talk to you, only him."

I thanked the vice president and hung up. To this day I have never received the courtesy of a reply or a telephone call from the National Cash Register Company. We later changed to another make of cash register and, perhaps, would have done so either way. NCR made our decision easier.

Our big objective was to open more stores. We heard about a store in North Wilkesboro that was going to become available, so I went up on a Friday and talked to the owner, Tal Pearson. He wanted to sell an entire strip shopping center: a warehouse, cafe, wholesale place and grocery store. I came back and talked with Brown and Wilson Smith, and they went up and looked it over on Sunday. We told Tal we would let him know something by Wednesday afternoon.

We came back to Salisbury and began drawing up the papers, but J. C. Faw, owner of Lowe's Supermarkets in North Wilkesboro, found out about our deal. He didn't want us as a competitor. He had tried to get Tal's store without offering him any real money because he knew Tal was going to prison for selling sugar to bootleggers. When he found out we were interested, he made Tal a better offer, including a certified check for $25,000 more.

"Well," Tal said, "I told the fellas they could have until Wednesday afternoon."

"You don't have anything signed, do you?" J. C. asked.

"No," Tal said, "a handshake to me is worth more than any signed paper."

Here was a guy with a grade school education going to prison for selling sugar to bootleggers, but his handshake was worth more than $25,000.

It was 12:01 p.m. Wednesday when J. C. came and said, "Ralph hasn't shown up yet, has he?"

"No," Tal said.

"Well, legally you've met your requirement," J. C. said. "It's Wednesday afternoon, and he's not here. You're free to accept my offer."

"Where I come from," Tal said, "afternoon lasts until dark."

We got up there around 3 o'clock and bought the store, but that wasn't our last run-in with J. C. Faw. We made a deal with Marsh Supermarkets of Indiana to buy a store in Hickory and intended to try a new concept: cost plus 10 percent. A David and Goliath operation in St. Louis was selling merchandise at extremely low prices and adding 10 percent at the checkout. It seemed like a good concept, so I went to take a look at it. While I was in St. Louis, Jim Berrier, our office manager, called.

"Ralph," he said, "forget about your trip. We're not getting the store in Hickory."

"What do you mean?" I asked.

"J. C. Faw got it," he said. "They just called and told me."

I called Marsh, and they said they had decided to give it to Faw. He had offered them more money. "I don't blame you," I told the Marsh people. "If he offered me more money, I would, too."

"No hard feelings?" the guy said.

"No," I said, "there's no hard feelings. Now I haven't talked to my attorney yet. I'm not sure. We're either going to sue you for $1 million or $2 million. I've got to get his expert advice on the amount. Rest assured, we're going to sue you because I've got a written document. I don't know if J. C. has one or not, but if he does, you're in trouble."

"Give me 30 minutes," the Marsh guy said.

He called back in 30 minutes and said the store was ours. We got the store ready to open, and the day before it opened we had advertisements in the newspaper. Brown called from Hickory.

"What would you say if I told you the Hickory store has a padlock on it?" he asked.

"Well," I asked, "how are you going to get out?"

"I am out," he said. "I'm at a pay station. J. C. Faw had a padlock put on it — a judge signed the papers."

I told Brown to hold tight. I'd get hold of J. C. Faw.

"I understand you had our store padlocked," I said to him on the phone.

"Yeah," he said, "Marsh promised me that store, and we're not going to let you in it. No hard feelings?"

"I'm glad to hear that," I said, "because there shouldn't be any. I want you to know you've made the mistake of your life. You've injured an innocent party. Your argument isn't with me or Food Town. Your argument is with Marsh. You should padlock their headquarters, not my store. I'm glad it's nothing personal because when I sue you it's nothing personal. I'm going to sue you for either one or two million dollars — the same amount I was going to sue Marsh for. I'll have to check with my attorney to see which one it is. You're going to lose. You've played hell this time."

"Give me 30 minutes," Faw said.

He called back and said he had found Judge Hayes, who had signed the papers putting on the padlock. "Wait a minute," he said, "you have to promise not to sue me if I get the padlock off."

"All right," I said, "if you get it off by 5 o'clock today."

The store started off as cost plus 10 percent, and we couldn't keep merchandise on the shelves. But people got confused about the 10 percent. Some thought it was 10 cents. Others didn't know percent from persimmons. The store started downhill and didn't stop. I literally tried to lose $2,000 a week by cutting prices and couldn't get customers. Boy, you're in trouble when you can't give away $2,000. Once something gets a bad name, it's hard to turn it around."

We had a new store in Statesville at that time, and it wasn't doing well either. I called J. C. Faw. "You've been wanting that store in Hickory all this time. Do you still want it?"

"Yeah," he said. "But I won't take the store in Hickory unless I can have the one in Statesville."

I would rather have gotten rid of the store in Statesville than the one in Hickory, but he didn't know that.

"No," I told him, "I don't want to let that Statesville store go."

Finally, he talked me into it.

The Hickory store eventually became home for a furniture dealer. J. C. couldn't make a go of it there either. When I found out he'd closed, I called him and told him he owed me for all the equipment. He hadn't read the lease. The equipment belonged to Food Town.

During those first 10 years we bought four stores in the Asheville area called Giezentanner's. We had hoped to buy some stores around Shelby called Tillman's, but he used our offer to go to Harris Teeter and get more money. We were determined to buy stores, so we ended up with four stores much farther away from our home base than we intended.

I had to travel quite a bit to Asheville to keep tabs on the stores, and one day I noticed a big billboard that said, "Take your wife out to dinner tonight." It had a picture of a man in a tuxedo and a lady in an evening gown, and they were seated at a table with candlelight. They were eating a beautiful steak.

The billboard was for Swift and Company, one of our major meat suppliers. I called Henry Gravely, head of Swift's North Carolina operations and a friend of mine.

"Henry," I said, "should we ever again decide to do business with your company, please, if you decide that you don't want our business, call me and let me know personally rather than letting me find out about it second hand."

"What are you talking about?" he said. "We highly value your business and certainly I do not want to lose it."

"Well, you have a billboard out on the highway that says don't shop at Food Town," I told him.

"I know it doesn't" he said, "but what are you getting at?"

"The sign says, 'Take your wife out for dinner tonight.' Obviously, if they take their wives out for dinner at a restaurant, then they cannot be eating food that came from Food Town, so, in effect, you are telling them not to trade at Food Town."

"I'll take care of that," Henry said.

The billboard was down within 24 hours. I never cease to be surprised and amazed at some of the poor thinking that goes behind some of the advertising and promotional ideas that I see."

Our venture in Asheville was just starting to go sour.

Part of the deal with the Giezentanner's — it's true with any agreement you ever make — was that the seller pays for any lawsuits that ever develop. You write that in every contract, because you don't want to be surprised with a lawsuit. We had those stores about six months when a meat packer billed us for 100,000 labels with Giezentanner's on them. We didn't want Giezentanner products so we refused to buy the labels. They sued Giezentanner's and named us as a co-defendant.

Our lawyer on retainer, Tam Shuford, gave me the name of a lawyer in Asheville, and I called him to represent us. We met a couple of times, and the date was set for the hearing. I went up for it. When I walked in the door, Harry Giezentanner said, "What are you doing here?"

That triggered alarms in my mind.

"I just came up for the day," I told him. The trial started at 10 o'clock. Lawyers went through all their rigmarole, and about 10 minutes to 3 the judge said they needed a recess. They didn't need a recess, but they recessed. My lawyer was going to the back with the judge, and I told him to be sure to get his money from the Giezentanners because they are obligated to pay for my attorney fees. "I'm not going to pay you a thing," I said.

They worked everything out. When it was over I asked the head man of the meatpackers, "Why did you sue us? We didn't have anything to do with it."

"We dropped the suit against you a long time ago," he said.

"You did WHAT?"

With that my lawyer looked at Giezentanner's lawyer and the Giezentanner lawyer said, "I told you about a month ago that Food Town is not a party to it any more." Then I knew why Harry asked "What are you doing here?"

I went out and wrote down exactly what was said, the time (4:34 p.m.) and the witnesses in case I ever needed it. In about six weeks I got a bill from the lawyer for $800. I called him and reminded him that he was to get his money from the Giezentanners.

"Yeah," he said "but they're not paying me. You've got to pay me."

I wasn't about to pay him. So he wrote me a letter and said if I didn't pay within 10 days he would enter suit. I called him the next day and told him to save nine days. "Go ahead and enter suit," I said. "Do it. Now I need a lawyer to represent me against you. How about you doing it? You be the lawyer for me and for yourself. You know all about it. I don't need to educate you or enlighten you on it. You know everything. You know you haven't got a case."

"I've never heard of such a thing," he said.

"Either you do that or forget it. If you proceed in this, I'm going to report you to the Bar Association and get you disbarred for not notifying me. You actually owe me money for my trip to Asheville. Here, let me read you what I've got written down about what the witnesses said."

That was one lawyer's bill that never got paid.

There were other problems with the Asheville stores. We lost quite a bit of money on them. But, as I always told my people, "If you've got lemons, make lemonade." They heard so much of that they got sick of lemonade.

Frank Outlaw was starting the Bi-Lo chain in Mauldin, S.C., and was moving into western North Carolina. I called him and told him I had four stores I would be interested in selling. We met at a motel in Morganton. He brought his lawyer and I took Tam Shuford. I told him I'd sell the stores at 17 percent off retail inventory. We were leasing the buildings, so that was not a problem.

"That sounds fair enough," he said. "How about the rent?"

"You can just take up the rent from the landlord," I said.

"I won't do that," he said.

"OK," I said, "I've got enough faith in your company that I'll take a percentage of your sales. Then I'll pay the rent, because I believe you're going to do well."

"You've got that much faith in me," he said, "then I'll pay you rent based on sales."

We shook hands and decided that we would sign the deal while there together, but the lawyers said they couldn't get it done that quickly.

"Ralph and I are going to go over here and have a cup of coffee," Frank said. "We want it finished when we come back. We all agreed. We sat here for 10 minutes and agreed on everything. Don't make it complicated. Just put down what we said."

We had a cup of coffee, and he bought the stores that day. It took a little time to take inventory, so I called Frank before he paid me and offered to take part of the $300,000 payment in Bi-Lo stock. Book value was about 70 cents a share, and I offered him $2.50 a share. "That's over three times what the book value is," I said. "If you ever need the money, you'll be tickled to death you did it, and if you don't need the money you won't miss that small amount of stock." He accepted my offer.

I went on the Bi-Lo board of directors, and Frank helped me out quite a bit. He helped me get used trucks when we couldn't afford new ones. We later sold that $100,000 worth of stock for $4 million when Bi-Lo sold out. That sounds good, but if we had invested in our own stock, that $100,000 would have been worth $40 million.

I wanted to lease a warehouse and was looking at a location owned by Enoch Goodman on U.S. 601 (now Jake Alexander Boulevard in Salisbury). He was to build and lease to us.

"Ralph," Enoch said, "one thing I overlooked. There's going to be a charge of $3,000 for tests on the soil to make sure it can hold a warehouse."

"Enoch, that's not my responsibility," I said. "It's your responsibility to make certain you give us a good solid foundation. I'm not going to pay the $3,000."

"Well," he said, "I won't do it."

The next day I found property nearby on Julian Road and bought it from W.A. Brown and Son Inc. About two days later, Enoch Goodman called and said, "You know, I've been thinking about that. You're right. That's my responsibility."

"Enoch," I said, "it's too late now. We have bought land on which to build."

"Your brother Glenn would have argued with me for weeks about that," Enoch said.

"Glenn's got money," I said. "If you don't have money you can't argue. You've got to move."

Stocking the warehouse was just as big a problem as building it. It wasn't long before we were expanding it and I wanted delayed dating on a shipment of merchandise from Campbell Soup Company. I asked my secretary, Katherine Clark, to call the vice president in charge of credit at Campbell. I told her to call him collect. A few minutes later she buzzed me and said that Mr. Fuester, Campbell's vice president, had refused to accept the call.

"Call him back and ask for the correct spelling of his name," I told her. "Tell him that I want to get it right when I call the president of the company to explain that the vice president had refused my call."

Katherine called back and — just as I thought — Mr. Fuester accepted the call. I picked up the phone and his first question was, "What do you mean by calling me collect?"

"You have a lot more money than I do," I explained. "If not, then you're in trouble. That's why I called you collect. I am your customer — you are not mine."

"I don't have to take that kind of stuff from you," Mr. Fuester said.

"No, you don't even have to talk to me. But if you hang up on me, I am going to call the president of Campbell Soup and tell him that you hung up on me."

That seemed to settle him down a bit.

"I know what you want," he snapped, "and the answer is no."

"You don't know what I want," I said. "If you did, the answer wouldn't be no. I want delayed dating, as I am moving into a new warehouse. I am entitled to delayed dating as I am duplicating stock for your benefit."

That wasn't 100 percent correct, as we were enlarging the warehouse rather than building a new one, but it did require the same consideration. Mr. Fuester said nobody else was giving me delayed dating, why should he?

"General Foods and General Mills were, along with others," I said.

"They are not," he said.

"Now I am going to hang up on you," I told him, "because you are calling me a damn liar. I am going to report you to the president."

"I did not call you a damn liar," he said.

"I added the 'damn' to make it sound better, but I am going to report you to the president if you insist on saying that I am lying to you."

He finally agreed that if General Mills and General Foods had granted me delayed dating, he would too. He wanted to call them himself to check it out. True to his word, he called me back.

"I don't know how you talked them into it, but both of them agreed that you can have the delayed dating," he said, "and we are going to grant it to you too."

Campbell Soup was so strong in its market share of soups, they got even tougher to deal with years later. In the summer when they packed tomato soup, they required their purchasers to buy all of their needs for approximately six to eight weeks, whether it be chicken noodle soup, macaroni and cheese, or any product. Campbell's felt that it would be so busy packing tomato soup, it wouldn't have time to ship any other products. This was in the late '60s, and Food Town needed seven carloads of Campbell's products to tide us over.

Campbell provided delayed dating on these advance shipments. That was one concession they were willing to make, because they needed to clear the decks for tomato soup. The Campbell Soup representative said that we could have just three carloads.

"Why?" I wanted to know.

"Mr. Fuester, vice president of credit at Campbell, said that was all you get," the salesman explained.

It all came back to me. The collect call five years earlier and all. I didn't bother calling collect this time. I got Mr. Fuester on the line and explained that Food Town's sales were up tremendously.

"No," he said, "three cars is all you get."

"Mr. Fuester, I don't believe you know who I am," I said.

"Yes," he answered, "you're Mr. Ketner."

"No," I said. "I'm that S.O.B. who called you about five years ago about delayed dating on a warehouse."

"Who are you again?" he wanted to know.

"I'm that S.O.B. with Food Town who called you and raised Cain because you didn't want to take my collect call and raised even more Cain when you didn't want to give me delayed dating."

"If you are that person," he said, "you can have all the carloads you want. You made me so mad that I watched your account for years hoping you would be late with a payment so I could get even. Your record is perfect. You have never been a day late with a payment."

"All that's well and good," I said, "but will you tell your salesman to let me have seven carloads of products?"

"You can have 10 carloads."

"Seven is all I want."

After the salesman hung up the phone with Mr. Fuester he was amazed. "That's the same guy who said you couldn't have but three cars yesterday."

"You didn't identify me properly as the S.O.B. Ketner, not just Mr. Ketner of Save-Rite, which was the name of our warehouse operation," I said.

In the early years after the number of stores peaked at 16 and started falling, we decided to use Merchant Distributors Inc., of Hickory as our supplier. Things worked out great for a few years, but MDI started pulling some things that I didn't like. They overcharged us on a few little things, and I found out they refused to handle some manufacturers' bargain offers because the markup was too small.

A guy came in one day and said if I would buy a case at $4, he would give me a case. "I'll take 400 cases," I said. "Ship it through MDI."

"They won't touch it," he said, "because they don't like anything to get down that cheap. Three percent on $2 is just 6 cents a case they'll get for handling it. If they pay full price of $4, they get 12 cents a case."

Policies like that just killed the merchants they were supplying. I had a meeting of a number of multiple-store operators and showed them these things. I said what we need to do is form our own warehouse and start a co-op because big operators are worth more than small operators. Only two wanted to go in with me. Oren Heffner of Mocksville, about 20 miles from Salisbury, operated three stores. Russell Walker of Asheboro, about 50 miles from Salisbury, operated six stores.

The three of us formed our own corporation to supply our stores with merchandise. We called the new company Save-Rite, and we invested in it according to the volume of each of our sales. Food Town supplied 40 percent; Russell Walker supplied 36 percent; and Oren Heffner put up the remaining 24 percent. I suggested Russell be president, Oren vice president and I would be secretary-treasurer and general manager. Titles didn't mean much to me, but I wanted to be in charge.

All our suppliers gave us delayed dating for our new warehouse without protest. They remembered past dealings with me through Food Town and Winn-Dixie.

Save-Rite's three partners got along fine until Russell Walker asked me to hire a friend of his as office manager. Within a few days, it was clear the fellow wasn't qualified. He knew little more than the difference between a credit and a debit. At our weekly meeting, I told Russell that his friend couldn't do the job, and I was going to let him go. He persuaded me to keep him on for a couple more weeks. He was confident that his friend could learn the job.

Four weeks later, I told Russell that the man simply had to go. This time, he agreed. A day later I had a call from Oren Heffner that he and Russell wanted to talk. They were at the Salisbury airport and would be right over. They walked in and, without so much as a good morning, Russell said, "Ralph, Oren and I have come to demand your resignation."

I asked him to repeat what he had just said. "This business is easy to handle," I told the two of them. "I refuse to resign. If you want me to resign, you'll have to vote me out."

I told Russell that as president he could make a motion that I be fired and I would second it. "Then I'll call the question which means, in case you don't know it, that there can be no further discussion, just a vote."

Russell made the motion that I be fired, and I seconded it.

"All those in favor of Ralph's being fired say 'aye'," Russell said. He voted "aye."

"All those against Ralph's being fired, vote 'no'," he said. I voted no.

So far there hadn't been a peep out of Oren Heffner.

"All right, Oren," I said, "it's up to you. The 40 percent ownership I control is on record against firing me. Russell had voted his 36 percent in favor of firing me. You decide whether I'm fired."

By this time, I was getting upset. And I let them have it with both barrels. "I don't know what brought all this about, but I want you to know that in the event Oren votes to fire me, I want you to get out of this office. It belongs to Food Town, not Save-Rite. I also want you to get your cars off this parking lot. It belongs to Food Town, too. I don't know whether the Food Town loading area is leased to Save-Rite, but I do know that neither of you knows how to run a wholesale grocery warehouse. And if you fire me, I'm immediately going to open another warehouse and hire all of your people away. They wouldn't want to work for somebody who doesn't know how to run a wholesale warehouse.

"Now you can think about all those things before you make up your minds on how Oren's going to vote on the motion to fire me."

Oren never had to cast his vote. Russell reconsidered, deciding it wouldn't be in his best interest to fire me. I suspect Russell got confused about the titles. Later I asked Oren what had caused him to agree to come with Russell and demand my resignation.

"It was as big a surprise to me," Oren said, " as it was to you, Ralph."

The three of us patched things up and operated as partners for several more years. We had occasional disagreements but settled them quickly. I made some mistakes in estimating what people would buy. One of my biggest blunders came when I purchased 200,000 plastic firetrucks in a close-out deal for seven cents each. The toys had been used as a promotion inside laundry detergent by Colgate-Palmolive-Peat, and I thought we could sell them for 10 cents. When I presented the firetruck idea to my partners, they wanted fewer than 5,000, leaving me with 195,000. I urged them to go all out on this, but we sold only 20,000. I was able to return about 160,000 of the firetrucks for a refund but continued to find boxes of them stored away in Food Towns for years. It seemed that every inventory for the next 10 years included plastic firetrucks carried over from the preceding year.

Another disagreement the Save-Rite partners had was over some cases of king-sized Fab I ordered without consulting them. Colgate-Palmolive was offering a very attractive deal, so I took 500 cases. Normally, we met on Wednesdays to decide what merchandise to order. My Food Town partner Wilson Smith usually represented me at those meetings. I made my pitch for the king-sized Fab as though I hadn't already ordered it.

Oren and Russell weren't interested. They didn't think it would sell. Neither did Wilson. I argued that they were all wrong — the price of the king size was as low as the price of the regular size, a box half its size. People were sure to buy it, I argued.

Wilson realized that I hadn't come to the meeting for my health. He said he would take 37 cases for our seven stores.

"I'll make it easy on you," I said. "I've got 500 cases in the warehouse, and you're going to get a minimum of 40 percent for our seven stores. I know they'll sell, and that's why I bought the detergent before the supply ran out."

I told Oren and Russell that if they were sure they didn't want any of the king-sized Fab, I'd take their allotments as well. They changed their minds and took the proportionate number of cases.

The huge boxes of Fab sold out in a matter of days, and my partners were calling to ask when they could get a new supply. I contacted Johnny McClamrock, the area Colgate-Palmolive representative, and told him to get us some more. He said there was no more available in his area. I told him to get off his fanny and look around the state for some. He found 1,000 cases, and we sold that quickly too. I called him back for more, and he said that he'd already looked all over North Carolina and there was no more available.

"Have you heard of the other 49 states?," I asked.

He found another 1,000 cases. That made 2,500 cases of detergent sold by 16 little grocery stores in North Carolina in a couple weeks. Johnny was recognized as Colgate-Palmolive Salesman of the Year — not bad for a man who didn't want to sell it in the first place.

Right there, I saw the excitement that could be generated by a box of detergent being sold at a bargain. The wheels began to turn. I was looking for a new idea.

6. Five Fast Pennies

Maybe you've heard the expression, "If you build a better mousetrap, the world will beat a path to your doorstep." Baloney. If you build a better mousetrap and don't learn to sell it, you had better learn to eat the darn thing.

In late 1967, I came up with a better mousetrap. How well we sold it and created excitement for it would ultimately determine whether Food Town went bankrupt or became a nationwide grocery chain.

Those first 10 years of "research and development" taught me a valuable lesson. You can't buy people's business — you've got to earn it. We had worked as hard as we could in our many promotions and pricing ideas. But in the end, we operated essentially as a "me, too" grocer. Food Town offered things such as weekend specials, trading stamps and sales prices tied in with minimum orders — but so did everybody else. We didn't really deserve to succeed. In 10 years, we had opened 16 stores and closed nine. Of the seven remaining stores, five were in Rowan County. Sales for 1967 were only $5.8 million and the earnings hardly registered at $36,061.

I was frustrated. I had put in 10 years of the hardest work I could imagine and really didn't have anything to show for it. And going into 1968, we projected our sales for the year at a 15 percent loss to $5 million. Things looked pretty dreary. I was looking for something that would cause customers to trade with us and not our competitors.

One day in November 1967, an article in "Progressive Grocer" caught my eye. The headline said, "How to build volume and make money with low-low prices," and the subhead said, "Turns loser into winner."

The loser turned winner was Robert Stragand, a grocer in Dayton, Ohio. By a strange coincidence, the name of his store also was Food Town. In this article, Stragand said he had reduced prices across the board and his sales had gone up tremendously. As I read further, I realized this fellow had the concept for which I was looking. But if a guy says he can run a four-minute mile, I want some proof. I told my wife, Ruth, I was heading for Dayton to see Stragand. I knew he would see me. Anytime you read something a guy has said in a newspaper or magazine, he's proud of it, and he'll talk to you.

I was right. I called him on a Monday, and I flew up to meet him the next day. I spent two to three hours listening and asking questions. He had cut the price on everything because of a conversation with a former customer. At church one Sunday, he asked a lady why he hadn't seen her in his store for the past two to three weeks. She answered that his prices were too high. Well, Stragand, a "me, too" operator himself, thought his prices were about the same as everybody's.

"You're two cents higher on Zweiback," the lady said.

Stragand was startled. He probably didn't sell five boxes of those crackers a week.

"I just started thinking," he told me. "If somebody knows that price, then 5,000 different people know 5,000 different items. So I just cut the prices on everything."

On the flight home, I was getting more excited by the minute. Stragand's store operated at the mercy of his wholesaler. He was paying for all the wholesaler's inefficiencies when he bought his goods. Food Town bought through Save-Rite and, as the buyer for Save-Rite, I knew we were operating efficiently. Buying through the warehouse also meant we had enough volume to receive good deals. Stragand's concept could actually work better for Salisbury's Food Town.

Within two days after returning from Dayton, I gathered up six months' worth of invoices from the warehouse, piled them into big cardboard boxes and took off to the Manger Motel in Charlotte. I had a bellman carry the boxes to the room. I also took an adding machine and card table. The bellman must have thought I was a bookie or something.

What I was doing was pretty simple, except I had to do it 3,000 times. I cut the price on every grocery item we sold out of the warehouse. If in six months I bought 100 cases of an item, it was a fair assumption that I sold all the cases. Say the item was a can of peas that I was reducing from 29 to 26 cents. That's 3 cents a can, 24 to a case, 72 cents a case and, if we moved 100 cases, I would figure a $72 loss. After 3,000 items, I added up the total losses. I think the Lord must have been with me because I never refigured my first calculations, which showed that my reductions would reduce Food Town's gross profit from 22 to 16 percent. The hard part was determining how much more volume would be needed to offset that.

But first I figured in some other factors. Each store had fixed expenses such as lights, depreciation, rent and other utilities — all the things that would stay constant regardless of the volume. Everything else would move in proportion to sales. If you double sales, you have to hire about twice as many people. The store manager's salary stays the same, so I factored that in. Certain supply costs go up. More volume would mean more paper bags, for example. After three days in that motel room, I figured we would need a 50 percent increase in sales just to break even. Now that's a heck of an increase against A&P, Winn-Dixie, Kroger and Colonial. I was hardly confident that we could do it, but I figured it was worth the gamble. Our first two weeks of sales in 1968 — when we were still a "me, too" operation — would bear me out. Projected over the whole year, it looked as if Food Town would lose money for the first time in its history.

But I had a selling job to do to the board, especially Wilson Smith.

"What happens if we don't meet your 50 percent projection?" he asked.

"Well, that's the easiest question anybody's going to ask me," I said. "We'll go bankrupt."

Wilson suggested that we try the concept in one store. If it didn't work, he said, then the whole company wouldn't go down the tubes. To me, we had had some great ideas in the past that we probably sabotaged by trying them only in one store. Our attempt at cost plus 10 percent at our Kash and Karry store in Hickory came to mind. I told the board I'd rather quit than try the low-price idea in just one store.

"I vote with you," board member Archie Rufty said. Archie was our only outside (non-employee) board member.

"Just like that?" I said, surprised at his support.

"Wait a minute," he said. "Let me ask a question. Do you own anything in the world other than Food Town stock?"

"You know I don't."

"Then I vote with you," Archie said. "You're willing to gamble everything you have in life on it. I'd be a fool not to go along with what you think is best."

Archie's support heartened me. Soon Bill Smith voted for the low-price concept, too.

Employees stood as our next selling job. The Sunday night before we began lowering every price in the stores we had a dinner for Food Town workers at Catawba College's Crystal Lounge.

"You think of any question that the customer might ask you, and you ask me so I can tell you how to answer," I told the employees that night. "Now we're going to have 77 salesmen in your stores, along with our people, cutting prices starting the first thing in the morning, And they're going to drastically cut the prices. But we're not going to have weekend specials. We're not going to have tie-ins with ten-dollar orders. And we're not going to have stamps."

The cashiers asked what their response should be when a customer complains about the price of Crisco. They might be able to buy it at Winn-Dixie for 99 cents with a ten-dollar order, while the Food Town price would be $1.19. What should they tell the customer?

"Tell them we're 20 cents higher," I said, "because we don't require you to buy ten-dollar orders to get that special. If you buy that ten-dollar order, you've probably spent $1.50 to save that 20 cents. Just tell the truth."

The salesmen came next. On the Monday morning after our Sunday dinner, we had a breakfast for 77 salesmen, representing national manufacturers. We asked them to spend the next three days helping us lower the price of every item in our stores. They even wore signs on their backs saying, "Pardon the inconvenience, I'm busy lowering prices for you."

The salesmen resented it. We were crazy, in their minds, for selling things such as baby food at carload cost, not even for a penny's profit. Dog food, the same. The salesmen knew their prices. They got disgusted and told me it wouldn't work, predicting they would be back in the stores within a couple of weeks changing the prices upward. The competition reacted pretty much the same way. Other stores thought we weren't going *out for business* — just going *out of business.*

They didn't understand. One key to the concept was that I was cutting prices on nationally advertised brands, which had our customers' confidence as quality products. Cutting prices on a lot of private label merchandise, which Food Town didn't have then, would not have worked. People would assume low cost meant poor quality.

The philosophy was, and remains, simple: *Five fast pennies are better than one slow nickel.* Food Town might sell five cans of beans with one-cent profit on each can to make a nickel. Other stores might sell one can of beans, to make the same nickel. But I'm stronger with more volume.

I was creating excitement through pricing. In the Charlotte motel room, I decided that one-sixth of everything in the warehouse — about 16 categories of items — would be sold at cost or less. Those items included baby food, sugar, cereals, grits, coffee, pet foods, shortening, rice and detergent. It's the kind of stuff a customer uses a lot, not something like a meat tenderizer. You're lucky to sell meat tenderizer to 20 customers a week. Pricing has to make an impression.

The low-price approach doesn't work with meat and produce. That is, Food Town remained competitive with other stores on meat and produce prices, but they were profit items. Once, during the 10 years of research and development, I decided Food Town would sell all of its meat at absolute cost. Our steak might be a dollar a pound or 50 cents a pound cheaper, but customers soon began equating low price with low quality. It only took a month or two before I realized selling meat at cost was a wild goose chase.

And produce didn't fit in with the pricing method. Today, tomatoes at 39 cents a pound may be extremely high-priced, but next week 79 cents a pound may be a low price. Because the market fluctuates, there's no such thing as a good price on lettuce or bananas. Anything that is perishable is subject to fluctuation, so it's hard for people to know they're getting a good price when the prices can change so much from week to week.

Again, it came back to low prices on nationally advertised brands.

Food Town advertised its move to everyday low prices as "The Big Change." It started on Jan. 18, 1968, and within a month or two, we knew low prices had struck a nerve with our customers. A conversation I had with Archie Rufty one day serves as a great example of what The Big Change was all about.

"You know what price you've got on Liquid Plunge, half a gallon?" he asked.

"Sixty-nine cents," I said.

"You mean to get that?"

"Yeah."

"Do you know what the competition gets?" Archie continued.

"A dollar sixty-nine."

"Do you mean to be a whole dollar cheaper? What do you get on quarts?"

"We don't carry quarts. The competition gets 89 cents for quarts. We sell a half-gallon for 69 — 20 cents less and twice the product. We don't need the quart."

"Do you really think you need to be a dollar cheaper?"

"Let me ask you one thing," I said. "Would you be happy if I had a 50-cent difference?"

"Yeah."

"Good, I won't do it."

"You just agreed with me," Archie protested..

"I didn't agree with you. You're excited about the dollar. You wouldn't be about the 50 cents. My whole concept is excitement and that's what we're building."

I tried to create as much difference as I could. Dog food is another example. Maybe it was supposed to sell at $1.99 a bag. We might get a deal on it and buy it at $1.19 a bag, but sell it in the stores for 99 cents and lose 20 cents a bag. But the customer saves a whole dollar. He goes home and tells his neighbors. We get more volume in the store, and we're stronger. You can't beat word of mouth.

One time, on a 25-pound bag of dog food, we were $2 cheaper than A&P or Winn-Dixie. We put up a sign in the stores that said, "With the $2 you save on this dog food, buy yourself a steak." That's merchandising. The whole idea of the game is that I'd rather have a poor idea with a lot of enthusiasm than the best idea with no enthusiasm.

But with this new idea, I didn't allocate much money on advertising, figuring out quickly that low prices were the best advertisement going. I remember, however, persuading *The Salisbury Post* reporter Ned Cline to write some copy for me to run in an advertisement. This was after he refused to write a business story for free, even though I told him my idea would revolutionize the grocery industry, *and it has*. He said it would be too much of a puff piece. Still, I managed to have him write a full-page "human-interest" story, which he insisted carry the small notation "PD ADV" at the bottom, signifying it was a paid advertisement.

Part of my argument with Ned was that if I invented a gasoline that would achieve 20 percent more mileage, effective immediately, he would love it.

"If I gave you the exclusive, you would hug my neck," I said. "Here I am telling you something that's going to save people 10 percent on their grocery bill, and you're just trying to ignore it."

I ended up paying Ned $300 for his work. I gave him the choice of $300 or $300 worth of Food Town stock. He's managing editor of the Greensboro News & Record these days and, believe me, he wishes he had taken the stock. By 1991, it would have been worth more than $5 million.

Sales increased almost overnight. After six months, they were up 35 percent. Still, I needed a big push to reach the 50 percent increase in sales Food Town needed by year's end, just to break even. I turned to two schoolteachers, Pat Barrow and Viola Dixon. I gave each of the women $100 to shop at a Winn-Dixie, A&P and Colonial. I told them to buy anything they wanted and, when they were finished, we would compare in a full-page advertisement, their costs at these other stores compared to what it would have cost at Food Town. It turned out we were roughly 16 percent cheaper than any of them. We ran a full page advertisement showing their pictures and results.

Up until this time, grocers had not singled out competitors by name, usually referring to them as stores X, Y and Z. I decided to call a spade a spade to lend credibility. The first Sunday after we ran the ad showing the results, one of our original investors, Cecil Kinder, saw me at First Presbyterian Church and mentioned to me that he feared that our competitors might sue us for having mentioned them by name. I said to Cecil, "The same thought entered my mind, but if they do, the only possible error that was in the ad was where I showed that one can of soup cost 13 cents whereas they sold it two-for-25 cents, which means that I overstated the cost by 1/2 cent.

"If they do sue me, I plan to run a full-page ad apologizing to them for saying they were $16 higher on a $100 purchase when, in reality, the true difference was $15.99-1/2. Cecil, I will get more mileage out of that ad than anything I could do."

You can rest assured that none of the three ever even thought about suing us.

For the next three months of summer, I paid Mrs. Barrow and Mrs. Dixon to knock on doors. They would ask people where they bought groceries, why they bought groceries there and so forth. They would always end by thanking the person for helping with their survey and, if the respondents were Food Town customers, they would inform them they were shopping at the low-price store. The glossy photograph, which they showed, supported the claim. It was no claim — it was true.

If the person listed Winn-Dixie, Colonial, A&P or some other store as his supermarket, either lady would say, "I think I owe it to you to tell you about a place to shop." They also gave out $2 gift certificates to Food Town. I met with the women every Saturday morning that summer and heard what they were finding out.

I learned something from Viola Dixon. She told me the people who don't trade with Food Town were either ignorant or stupid. I thought the two words meant the same thing, but she corrected me.

"A person who has heard of Food Town and doesn't trade with you, that's stupidity," she said. "A person who has never heard about Food Town, that's ignorance.

Their surveys that summer revealed that lower-income people were slower to convert to Food Town shoppers, even though Food Town would have saved them money. I've also noticed over the years that Country Club residents are among the first to begin shopping at Food Lion. There's a prestige to being smart, and Food Town gradually became a prestige place to shop for the smart people looking to save money.

I don't know exactly what impact the two schoolteachers had on sales for the rest of 1968. I like to think they helped a lot, as did a new slogan for the pricing concept. A couple of months into the changeover, somebody told me, "You know, you've got the lowest prices in North Carolina." I started toying with the phrase and decided to borrow the first letters from "Lowest Food Prices in North Carolina" and came up with LFPINC. Someone seeing it for the first time naturally asked what the letters stood for, and it sort of reinforced the message. We had thousands of bumper stickers printed up, and LFPINC became our rally cry for years to come.

Another important ingredient linked to the pricing was the efficiency of Food Town's operation. Since we established Food Town in 1957, and for sure since 1968, I would say we've been, by far, the low-cost operator in our industry. When you sell for less, you can do it by one of two ways: operating for less or buying for less. Ours is a combination of the two. Suppose you gave Rembrandt and me the same paint. He might use the paint to create a beautiful piece of art. I would make a mess. Our competitors used to mishandle buys in a lot of situations. They're getting better. But it also costs them more to operate. In terms of buying and operating, even back in 1968, we were Rembrandt.

We did things differently. Even today, Food Lion doesn't use zone pricing, which is another way of saying "charging what the traffic will bear." We have one store in Rockwell, North Carolina. It's the only grocery store in town. The prices there are the same as those in the competitive Charlotte market. I've never believed that you should charge a customer more for groceries just because you have the only supermarket in town.

There's plenty of evidence that Food Lion's presence in a market has caused grocery prices to come down. A year after we entered Jacksonville, Florida, a newspaper there stated that a survey showed grocery prices had dropped six percent. The grocery market of Jacksonville is $850 million per year. People there saved $51 million a year on groceries after we arrived. This has proven to be true in every area we've moved into.

Another thing that made us unique was my decision years ago not to raise the price of an item once it was marked and on the shelf. If the price went up, we sold the remaining stock at the old price. If the price went down — that didn't happen very often — we would reduce the old price. Under this policy, we would sometimes have two prices on the shelf at the same time, but we educated our customers to the fact that the lower price was to their advantage. If a customer wanted a can of beans, for instance, and saw the price was going up, she might buy several cans at the lower price. This helped us rotate the stock and helped our shoppers save money. After Food Lion began using price scanners the idea lost its impact because all items on the shelf had to have the same price in the computer. We kept the principle by waiting several days before raising prices when costs went up.

During the time that President Nixon was in office, there was a price freeze on all items in the grocery industry. I did not bother to read the fine print of the law, as I knew that our policy of never raising a price until we paid more for the product was much more severe than anything the government could dream up.

By now, you've probably determined that Food Town increased its sales by 50 percent in 1968. Sales came in at $8,958,916 — a 54 percent increase over 1967. In my mind, sales actually had increased 80 percent. Remember, if we had not gone to LFPINC, our projected sales in 1968 were $5 million. LFPINC also led to a $95,463 profit, a 165 percent increase from 1967. We ended the year with nine stores, but the sky seemed the limit.

As you can imagine, I became obsessed with everyday low prices: Instead of standing back and being satisfied with how

FOOD LION, INC.
COMPARISON 1967 - 1992

Year	Sales (000)	% Increase	Net Income (000)	% Increase	Return on Beg. Equity	Nbr. of Stores Year/End
1967	$ 5,815	--	$ 36	--	6%	07
1968	8,959	54%	95	165%	15%	09
1969*	15,320	71%	326	241%	45%	09
1970	22,397	46%	411	26%	33%	12
1971	36,996	65%	888	116%	39%	15
1972	50,251	36%	1,270	43%	38%	17
1973	71,373	42%	1,617	27%	31%	19
1974	92,481	30%	2,067	28%	31%	22
1975*	129,986	41%	3,752	81%	38%	30
1976	173,108	33%	4,861	30%	36%	45
1977	218,987	27%	5,789	19%	30%	55
1978	299,267	37%	9,481	64%	38%	69
1979	415,974	39%	13,171	39%	39%	85
1980*	543,883	31%	15,287	16%	33%	106
1981	666,848	23%	19,317	26%	32%	141
1982	947,073	42%	21,855	13%	28%	182
1983	1,172,459	24%	27,718	27%	28%	226
1984	1,469,564	25%	37,305	35%	30%	251
1985	1,865,632	27%	47,585	28%	29%	317
1986*	2,406,582	29%	61,823	30%	30%	388
1987	2,953,807	23%	85,802	39%	32%	475
1988	3,815,426	29%	112,541	31%	33%	567
1989	4,717,066	24%	139,775	24%	32%	663
1990	5,584,410	18%	172,571	24%	32%	778
1991	6,438,507	15%	205,171	19%	31%	881
1992*	7,195,923	12%	178,005	(13%)	22%	1012

* 53-Week Year

Notes:
1 - "LFPINC" started in 1968.
2 - Company founded in 1957 was first publicly traded in 1970.
3 - Extraordinary gains in 1970 - 72 and 1977 have been excluded.
4 - STOCK SPLITS: 1963 - 4 X 1; 1970 - 5 X 1; 1972 - 2 X 1; 1976 - 3 X 1; 1979 - 3 X 1; 1982 - 3 X 1; 1983 - 2 X 1; 1986 - 3 X 1; 1987 - 2 X 1; 1992 - 3 X 2 = 19,440 shares for one original 1957 share.

Food Town had turned around, I looked for more prices to cut. The thing just fed on itself.

One night — really about 1 o'clock in the morning — I was working at my kitchen table at home.

"When is this going to stop?" Ruth asked.

"What do you mean?" I answered.

"You know what I mean."

"Yeah. But if I weren't here working, what would we be doing? Playing bridge?"

"Well, yes," she said.

"Same time. Same thing. What's the problem?

"I would be enjoying it."

"Have you ever grabbed hold of a bear and tried to let go?" I asked. "This thing is so good. This concept is working so good, I can't let go of it. It'll run over me in a minute, because I'm the only one who can drive. I've got to stay ahead of it, if it takes 24 hours a day straight through."

And I did.

7. Go-Go '70s

In 1970, Food Town was like a rocket waiting to blast off. We knew our LFPINC concept worked, and we added three stores that year. That doesn't sound like a lot, but it's 25 percent. Then we added two, then three, then eight, then 15, 10, 14, 16, 21.

In other words, we tried to grow at 20 to 25 percent a year. In 1975 we grew from 30 to 45 stores. There was no pattern, only that we became more confident that our concept was the answer, and just as fast as we found locations, we took them.

It was 1970 that I made one of the decisions that led Food Town to becoming America's fastest growing grocery chain. I hired Tom Smith as a buyer. I was working 100 hours a week and was desperately looking for the right man to help take over the buying and warehouse operations. But the longest anyone had lasted was three weeks. People would make mistakes. "Ninety-eight was failing with me," I'd tell them. "If you make errors 2 percent of the time, you're gone."

I had one kid who could have made it, a fellow named Brown from Granite Quarry, but he came in after two or three weeks and said he wanted to quit.

"Why?" I asked. "You're doing a good job."

"I come in in the morning," he said, "and you're here. It doesn't make any difference what time I leave in the evenings, and you're here. I just don't want to work for anybody that works as hard as you do, because you expect it of me."

"That's right," I said. "Let me tell you something. I probably will make more money than you ever will. But you may be happier. I get happiness out of work. You haven't learned that yet, but I love to work. You need a job 8 to 5. You'll be with your family, be with your kids and everything. Your route's different than mine. We walk to the beat of a different drum."

He was good, but a lot of the others I hired were misfits.

My former wife, Ruth, actually suggested hiring Tom Smith. He had been with Food Town before and now worked for Del Monte. Tom grew up in China Grove, just a few miles from Salisbury, and had been a bag boy in one of our Salisbury stores and rose to manager of our store in Kannapolis. He worked his way through Catawba College and took a job with Del Monte, the big fruit and vegetable company. It was no easy selling job to get Tom to listen to my offer.

"I've worked for you before," he said. "I don't have any interest."

I had to talk fast. This was the new Food Town. LFPINC was revolutionary and there was a great future here. Finally, Tom agreed to meet me at a restaurant before an Army Reserve meeting. I offered him a stock option — the first in company history — and the chance to become the next president of Food Town. I was hiring him as a buyer and hoping that he would become president. Later we offered stock options to store department managers and up. However, the three founders, Brown, Wilson, and myself *never* had a stock option.

"What's the longest anybody has ever lasted with you?" he asked.

"Three weeks," I told him. "But most don't make it that long. The pace is too fast and the work's too hard. With me, 98 is failing."

"How will we get along in terms of our personality?" Tom asked.

"We'll either love each other," I said, "or one of us will leave. And the one to leave won't be me."

Tom wanted to think about it overnight. He called the next day. "I'm your man," he said.

He analyzes everything to the Nth degree. He's done an excellent job. I would still be working 100 hours a week if it weren't for Tom Smith because you can't delegate until you get the right man. It's suicide to delegate to the wrong person. I hope Tom knows this, and I hope I wasn't wrong about Tom.

Tom isn't the type to bet the company. Now I wouldn't want him there if he was going to bet the company. It was a different ball game in 1968 when we bet on LFPINC. It wasn't much of a company. Tom has been able to continue building on my concept.

Tom can be tough when he needs to be, and that's a necessity in this business. I got some proof of that by accident at a food dealers convention in Florida a few years later. I was sitting with Tom's former boss at Del Monte, Bob Whitis. We overheard some people at a nearby table discussing what a rude S.O.B. Tom Smith was.

"Bob," I said, "could they be talking about my Tom Smith?"

"I've got a feeling they are," he said.

I went over to the table where we'd heard the remarks about Tom and asked if they had been talking about Tom Smith of Save-Rite of Salisbury.

"Yes, he's the one," a man said. "Do you know him?"

"As a mater of fact, I do," I said. "He's vice president of my company and heads up our buying and warehousing operation."

"Well, I've never talked to anybody that rude and demanding in my life," the man, who identified himself as a vice president of a food processing company, said.

"I'll talk to Tom about this," I said. "He certainly shouldn't have done that."

The guy thanked me for my attitude about the matter.

"Don't misunderstand me," I said. "I'm not going to criticize Tom for being rude. I'm going to get on him for wasting time talking to vice presidents. I've always told him to go straight to the president, and I'm going to give him hell for not doing it this time."

"He would have talked to the president," the man said, "but the president wouldn't talk to him. He has more sense than to deal directly with Tom Smith. That's why the call came to me."

That was music to my ears.

Food Town was growing so fast, we needed more money. In 1969, Glenn Anderson of Carolina Securities of Raleigh sold $275,000 worth of debentures for us. They were convertible to common stock and paid 6 percent interest. Within a year, sales were going up so fast we decided to call them in. It was risky, because we didn't have the money to call them all, but I felt that people would say to themselves, "If they're calling these things in five years early, they know something really good. We'd better keep them. If we could convert them to common stock, we wouldn't have to pay the interest, and, since we paid no dividend, we could use that money for free."

About 90 percent of the holders of the debentures did convert. One man from Hickory wrote that he had been out of town and didn't get the letter. "You can not refuse to let me convert because I've been out of town," he wrote. We gladly agreed.

The next year we had our first, and only, public offering. Parker-Hunter of Pittsburgh handled it for us, and they say Food Town has been the best issue they've ever had as far as growth.

You used to hear about Winnebago and now Wal-Mart. We've outperformed all of them. A few years ago, I saw some numbers listing the fastest growing Dow Jones industrial stocks from 1933. Had you invested $10,000 in 1933 it would have grown to $816,000 by 1988. If you had invested the same $10,000 in Food Town in 1957 (24 years later) it would have been worth $142 million in 1988. And today it would be worth over $135 million. We've outperformed them over 160 to 1.

We went public to raise more money, and at the time we had grown from seven stores to 12. People say it gets harder to open 100 stores a year. It's hard if you only have 100 stores. That's a 100 percent increase. But if you have 1,000 that's a 10 percent increase.

The (re)tail of two cities

E very now and then, exciting things happen in Salisbury. The new telephone books arrive. Someone opens a new restaurant. And Food Lion stocks starts going up in price.

Many miles away, the residents of Bentonville, Ark., find excitement in the same simple pleasures. But the pulse of Bentonville folks quickens at the mention of Wal-Mart, not Food Lion. For Bentonville is to Wal-Mart, what Salisbury is to Food Lion —headquarters.

It's amazing how similar these two companies are.

Price, satisfaction

A basic Wal-Mart tenent has been that there's no substitute for customer satisfaction. A Wal-Mart employee once noted that "if he (a customer) goes away mad, he'll knock off a dozen customers." Food Town (later Food Lion) employees have long observed the same philosophy. "If you're going to make it good, don't make them mad," one former executive recalled as his marching orders.

The companies' approaches to buying and distribution are the same. Buyers demand the best possible deals and concessions from manufacturers and vendors. Why? So the savings can be passed on to the "everyday low prices" in each chain.

Both companies build huge warehouses close to stores so distribution is quick and the drive time of trucks is kept at a minimum. Wal-Mart and Food Llon strive for high productivity and low overhead. Their cost of doing buiness is the lowest for their respective industries. To save money, they are fanatics about little things, like turning lights off or recycling.

Both retailers solicit ideas for saving money from their employees and reward the people with good ideas. Management is demanding. The companies drive employees to succeed through quick advancement, pay and benefits, if they prove adaptable to the fast pace and ever-changing nature of their jobs.

Each of the firms relies heavily on corporate planes as essential travel tools. Through the years, head-to-head competitors have paid each company the high compliments of adopting low-price structures.

Wal-Mart has made daring invasions of the Northeast in its growth. Food Lion has taken similar chances with its pushes into Florida, Texas and Pennsylvania. Both companies have strong anti-union positions.

Nothing showy

Food Lion and Wal-Mart have built much of their success with stores in small towns. They keep their large corporate offices austere and functional, nothing showy. Sam Walton, the man behind Wal-Mart has been called an old yard rooster who loves a good fight—a promoter "in the P.T. Barnum style." The same could easily be said for Ralph Ketner, Food Lion's chairman emeritus.

Wal-Mart first went public with its stock in 1970—same year as Food Town. Wal-Mart has had eight two-for-one stock splits since then. Food Lion also has had eight stock splits since 1970, but they included a five-for-one split, four three-for-one splits and three two-for-one splits.

Wal-Mart's investors have seen 400 shares in 1970 grow to 102,400 shares by 1990. A Food Lion investor has seen 400 shares in 1970 grow to 1,296,000 shares in the same period.

Stock analysts frequently refer to Food Lion as the Wal-Mart of grocery stores. It would be just as easy, and maybe even more correct, to call Wal-Mart the Food Lion of discount department stores. So there, Bentonville.

—**Mark Wineka**
Associate editor

By the beginning of 1972, we were getting so crowded in the warehouse on Julian Road, it was becoming inefficient. In April, I was riding on Harrison Road and saw a sign "This Property For Sale." I called and the owner said he wanted $150,000. "We'll take it," I said.

"Just like that?" he said. "You don't have to ask anybody?"

"No," I said. "I'll send you a check for $5,000 as earnest money."

"You don't have to do that," he said. "I'll get the papers ready."

"No," I insisted, "I'm going to send you $5,000 so you know we really mean business."

About a week later the man called and said he'd been offered more money for the property.

"I expected that," I said. "The minute word got out I was interested, the price was going up. Did you get my check?"

"Yes," he said, "but I'm not legally bound because we haven't signed anything."

"I'll buy that," I said. "Morally, yes. Legally, no."

"I wish you hadn't said that," he answered.

The moral question won out. We got the property and began building a new warehouse and office building.

We took the low bidder on the warehouse, trying to save some money, but we hired a local architect to inspect the pouring of footings and everything to make sure the contractor was complying.

The day they finished pouring the concrete floor in the warehouse, Tom and I came by and noticed 25 boxes of steel mesh out in front. I knew exactly how many freight bills we had for steel mesh, and I knew they were supposed to be in that concrete floor. The next morning they were gone, and I knew what had happened. The contractor came and picked them up.

We still owed some money on the final payment. "I'm not going to pay you," I told the contractor.

"What do you mean?" he said.

"You didn't put the steel mesh in there as required in the specifications."

"Yes, I did."

"You had 25 boxes left over."

"Oh, no. There couldn't have been."

"I'll tell you what I'll do," I told him. "I'm so sure you knew about it, that I'm going to agree to take a lie detector test. I owe you $20,000, and I'm not going to pay you. That's up front, unless you take the lie detector test. Now if you take it and pass it, I'll pay you $40,000. If I take it and fail, I'll give you $40,000. But if I'm telling the truth and you're lying, I'm not going to pay you anyway. So you've got nothing to lose."

"No," he said, "I'm not going to take it. It's the principle of the thing."

We later found that we had overlooked putting the steel poles at the end of each aisle to keep a fork lift from running into the racks. In drilling for the poles, we found concrete three inches thick in some places. It was supposed to be six inches thick everywhere. I was about to kill the architect. He hadn't checked anything.

I learned my lesson from that experience, and several years later saved thousands of dollars by checking on an attorney representing us when the City of Salisbury wanted to annex the Harrison Road warehouse.

It was a foregone conclusion that the city would annex the warehouse, but I told our attorney, who was on a retainer since we did not have an attorney on the company payroll at that time, that I wanted all the books he had on North Carolina annexation laws. I wanted to become an expert on it.

127

Food Lion's philosophy: Buy more for less and buy it all out of one location. Corporate headquarters on Harrison Road in Salisbury, and the building as it's dwarfed by huge warehouse in aerial photo, above. *Photos courtesy of The Salisbury Post.*

I read in *The Salisbury Post* on June 27 that the city planned to annex our warehouse and other property on July 1. I immediately called our attorney and told him that he had three days to appeal the annexation process. He explained to me that the law permitted 30 days. I explained to him that if you appealed before the effective date, July 1, then you would not pay any taxes until after all appeals. That could take two or three years. If you did not appeal prior to the effective date, you had to begin paying taxes immediately and continue paying them through the final appeal. If you won the case, the city had to refund the money. If you lost — and I was certain we would lose — you got nothing back. Of the nine or 10 attorneys involved in the annexation case, ours was the only one who filed an appeal within the three-day period. Naturally, the city permitted other parties to ride on our coattails, and, as a result, we saved $600,000 to $700,000 in taxes.

Ted Law of the Better Business Bureau of Charlotte came to see me one day.

"Mr. Ketner," he said. "You're doing a wonderful job. You're doing this and that .... Everything's beautiful. We want you to join the Better Business Bureau in Charlotte."

"Ted," I asked, "what will that cost?"

"Five hundred dollars."

"My gosh," I said, "for $500 I can lower some more prices."

He took my refusal personally. He criticized us for saying we had the lowest prices in North Carolina. If somebody had a lower price on a penny box of matches that disqualified us from using that slogan, he said. We had quite an argument over it.

I wrote him a letter: "In *The Charlotte Observer* this morning, it says Harris Teeter is the friendliest store in town. Now I'm sure you checked it out, and they do have the friendliest store. What kind of gauge did you use to measure their friendliness? Are they 10 percent friendlier than we are or just five percent friendlier? Obviously, you wouldn't let them say that without being critical of them.

"Now here's another one. This fellow says he has the widest gun selection in America. How many guns does he have? And what is the second most? If the other guy buys more guns, can he use that? Obviously, you've checked that out."

And I went through 20 different things in the newspaper.

"Now Ted," I wrote, "I'm sure you've checked all of these things out. But if you haven't, and I'm sure you haven't, now that I'm calling them to your attention, you must. You can't, in your hometown, let these people go. I'm over here in Salisbury. I'm not even bothering anybody in Charlotte."

One day soon afterward, my son Robert was visiting me at the office and a reporter from *The Charlotte Observer* called. I talked to the guy for 45 minutes, and when I hung up Robert asked why I had taken such great pains with him.

"Son," I said, "tomorrow he's going to run something in the newspaper that can be for me or against me. Now so far, he's only heard Ted Law's side. I've got to explain to him what really happened, and I've got to keep explaining it to him as long as he'll let me talk to him."

The next day *The Charlotte Observer* had the story on the front page.

I told Robert: "Even though you know you're right, you're not right in the eyes of the other person until he agrees you're right. You've got to keep talking to that person as long as he'll let you."

Television reporters are different. You can talk 15 or 20 minutes and it will be cut to 15 seconds that night. Big Star ran an ad saying they were closing their stores and cutting prices to match ours. A TV reporter wanted my reaction.

"Up until now," I said, "the only place I've read about miracles has been in the *Bible*. Now I'm seeing one."

"What do you mean?" he asked.

"A competitor is running a full-page ad saying to customers, 'Look, we've been overcharging and cheating you for years, but because of Food Town we're going to do better and reduce prices. It's not for your benefit, but because they forced us.' Now that's a miracle. It's unbelievable that people would come out and admit they've been cheating and overcharging people."

Of course, none of that ended up on television.

We have had a lot of fun with our competitors through the years, although I'm not sure they always appreciated our sense of humor. A&P once ran a newspaper ad claiming the lowest over-all prices. We countered with an ad that had a big picture of a pair of overalls and the words "A&P claims they have the lowest overall prices. Food Town doesn't sell overalls, so we don't know whether A&P has the lowest overall prices. We do know that Food Town has the lowest food prices. Therefore, if you want food, there's only one place to shop: Food Town. If you want overalls, we suggest you check out A&P."

Once LFPINC caught hold, we stopped using games and gimmicks to get customers, but I noticed that Winn-Dixie, Colonial Stores and A&P were all sponsoring cash prize games at the same time. I studied their ads and drew up a letter for our advertising manager to run in the local papers. It was addressed: "To Whom It May Concern." The ad asked if readers had noticed that Food Town's competition had turned to luring customers on the chance of winning money. If the reader wanted to play games for money, I said, he ought to go to Las Vegas, where the chances of winning would be much better.

The law requires anyone running a game with prizes of money to print the odds against winning. The type was so small, it was nearly impossible to read without a magnifying glass. I was providing a service by printing the odds in type big enough to read and explaining what it meant. A person entering a Winn-Dixie store offering a $2,000 prize had one chance in 255,111 to win the money. If he shopped once a week at this store, chances are it would take nearly 4,905 years to become a winner. To win, I pointed out, a customer at that Winn-Dixie would have had to start shopping there 3,000 years before Christ.

Albert Gubay, who had made $30 million in England when he sold a grocery operation, decided to take on Food Town in the late '70s with a new operation called "3 Guys."

He had built a 400,000 square foot warehouse before he opened his first store. That's not too sensible, but he tried to make a big splash by burning $10 bills on his television commercials and telling people they were wasting money shopping at conventional grocery stores. He claimed his warehouse concept was going to put us all out of business.

His first store in Charlotte had a big banner reading, "Opening soon, with prices lower than LFPINC." He was coming after Food Town.

One day my secretary said that somebody from Charlotte radio station WSOC wanted me to be on a panel discussion with A&P, Winn-Dixie, Harris Teeter and Albert Gubay. I agreed to do it, but when I got there for the radio show it was just Albert Gubay and two of his lawyers.

"Where's A&P, Winn-Dixie and Harris Teeter?" I asked.

"It's just you and Mr. Gubay," the radio announcer said. "They were never supposed to be here."

My secretary took everything down in shorthand when she talked to people on the phone. I knew she had been told the others would be part of the panel. I had been set up.

"Do you want to be on the air or not?" the reporter asked. "He's got a full hour. If you want to be on there with him, you go."

"He's had two weeks to prepare," I argued. "But I'll try to handle it."

"Do you two people dislike each other?" was the first question asked.

"I don't know," I said, "I just met him. How do I know whether I like him or dislike him?"

Mr. Gubay said about the same thing, but he turned up the heat pretty quickly after that. He wanted to know if 3 Guys opened with lower prices than Food Town would we take down our LFPINC signs.

"It all depends," I said, stalling for time to try and think of something to say. What does it depend on? I'm thinking.

"It all depends on why you do it," I said. "You've been quoted in the newspaper that you have so much money your biggest problem is spending the interest on the interest. Now I don't have that problem. We have to work for everything we make, so if you have so much money that you can deliberately lose money to put us out of business, no, I won't give you any brownie points for that.

"It's for selfish reasons, so you can jack your prices up the minute you get us out of business."

It went on for an hour like that. We had a break at 12:30 for the news, and the reporter turned to us and said, "The phone's been ringing like it's going out of style."

"I go in your stores," Gubay said, "and you claim that you don't raise the price on anything once it's marked. You've got two prices on a bunch of items."

"That's right," I said. "Thanks for proving my point. If we had the same price, then obviously you would know that we've changed prices. But the two prices means it's going up, and we'll let the customers buy at the old price before they pay the higher price."

People asked me later how I thought I did against Gubay on the show. I would give myself 49 out of 100 points with him getting 51, but he had two weeks to prepare. He was pulling out figures, quoting things. "You've got so and so at your store. You did this and that." But it was a lot better than if it had been just him on the radio. He was smart and really came across well on television. He made his survey results available to the stations, and they used some of them. I told them they were just giving him free publicity. "Now you can be a fool," I told them, "but how long are you going to be a fool? He's a lot smarter than you are." We finally got through to the station manager, and they cut him off.

Within seven years, 3 Guys had gone broke. Gubay left before that, selling the whole operation to a few of his vice presidents. He said he had made the biggest mistake of his life in coming here and going head to head with Food Town because his concept would have worked anywhere else in the United States and it probably would have.

Several times I tried to get together with J. C. Faw and merge Food Town and Lowe's Foods, and in 1976 we actually went as far as the Federal Trade Commission, which opposed us. J. C. and I went to the hearing with our lawyer, and the FTC sent five lawyers to fight it. Their whole argument was that it would be restraint of trade.

"In preparation for this meeting today," the judge said, "I visited two Food Town stores and two Lowe's stores. I know the prices, gentleman, and it would be the greatest thing that ever happened to the customers of Lowe's to have Food Town's prices."

The judge ruled in our favor, but the lawyers from Washington said they wanted to appeal. The judge said his ruling was final, but they said Section so and so said they could appeal.

"All right," the judge said, "I'm going to make it easy on you. You've got until Monday morning (this was Friday afternoon) to find a judge who will hear your case."

They already had a judge lined up, and he killed the merger. We've always felt that one of our competitors had some input into that.

J. C. got so angry about what the judge said about the prices, he suggested we just call the whole thing off any way. I agreed. It turned out to be the best thing for us, because he would have owned so much stock he would have been able to influence decisions and kill some of our growth.

Today, Food Lion is recognized as the fastest-growing supermarket chain in the United States, but we had a hard time getting much recognition in the 1970s. In June 1978, South magazine had a cover story regarding the 10 outstanding growth companies in the Southeast. I eagerly turned inside the magazine to read the article because I felt that Food Town would be No. 1. Imagine my surprise when we were not one of the top 10 or even among the second 10 although we had outperformed the No. 1 company two-to-one.

"I read with much interest and disbelief your article regarding the 10 outstanding growth companies in the Southeast," I wrote the publisher of South magazine. Food Town outperformed your top company two-to-one, and yet we are not listed in the top 20. How is this possible? It is obvious that I do a much better job of increasing sales and earnings than I do in communicating with publications such as yours and will try to do better in the future."

About a week later, I received a letter from the publisher stating that our results were tremendous, and he was just sorry that the panel of judges did not consider Food Town, but that the blame for not making the list was not South magazine but the panel of experts, which consisted of eight or ten brokerage firms. He gave me a list of names and addresses and I wrote them a letter similar to the one I had written the magazine's publisher, closing with the thought "I apologize for my failure to keep you properly informed in the past and assure you that I will try to do a better job of communicating in the future."

Thirty days went by, and I did not receive a reply from a single one of the panel of experts. I wrote each of them again with a carbon copy going to the publisher of South magazine. I told them that I wanted to change the last paragraph of the original letter apologizing for my failure to communicate.

"I have not received the courtesy of a reply from any of you," I wrote, "therefore, it is obvious that you have a problem of either reading or writing. In view of this, it is impossible for me to communicate. Therefore, I withdraw my apology."

The following year on the cover of South magazine was a picture of Ralph Ketner standing in front of one of our cash registers with a banner hanging in the background stating: "Food Town Everyday Low Prices."

Inside was an article in which I said, "I was thinking one morning while I was shaving, 'Why doesn't everyone shop at Food Town?' The answer is that they are damn fools, but you can't say that on television."

I have the picture from the magazine and the story on my office wall in the Ketner School of Business at Catawba College. I did receive a letter from a shareholder who took exception to my quote regarding people being damn fools. She said that she did not feel that the CEO of a company should use such language, and that she questioned being involved as a shareholder because of my profanity. I wrote and explained to her that my use of the word damn was not meant to be profanity, but was perhaps an indication of my limited vocabulary. If she felt this strongly, I said, she could ask her broker to refund her original investment and pay her 12 percent compounded interest. I was positive the broker would comply. Her investment had grown at 25 to 30 percent a year. I never heard anything further from the lady.

Food Town had plenty of doubters. My former partners Russell Walker and Oren Heffner turned down the chance to merge with Food Town.

"It's impossible for me to imagine how much money I'd be worth," Oren said, "but, in hindsight, I don't believe you would have done as well. We wouldn't have let you do what you did. You had nobody to put the brakes on you."

I thrive on change, and one of the most dramatic changes we made was in our name. It was 1983, and we were going into

Tennessee. We found that there were about 100 stores operating under the name Food Town. They were independent but advertised jointly. They had rights to the name.

I was riding down the road one day and suddenly snapped my fingers.

"What's wrong?" my wife asked.

"I just thought of the new name for Food Town," I told her.

"I didn't know you were going to change it," she said.

"Well," I said, "we hadn't really decided, but our logo is the lion and we can change our name from Food Town to Food Lion by buying just two letters: "L" and "I" and using the old letters "O" and "N" from TOWN to spell the new name."

We had 100 stores, and it cost $500,000 to change the name. Some people warned us about using the lion as our symbol. People might not think we were going to be as friendly. But it doesn't matter what your name is. If you sell merchandise people want at a price that's lower than your competitors, you will be successful.

And, I thought, we'd never have the problem of bumping into another grocery chain with the same name as ours.

8. Buon Giorno, Belgians

By 1974, it was evident that LFPINC could make Food Town a regional and, no doubt, national grocery chain some day. I knew it. All you had to do was look at the numbers.

Remember, sales in 1968 increased 54 percent to $8.95 million, and earnings went up dramatically to $95,000. That was just an omen of things to come. By the end of 1973, sales had grown to $71.3 million, and earnings had increased to $1.6 million. From seven stores in 1967, Food Town had grown to 19 stores by the end of 1973. The stock split five-for-one in 1970 and two-for-one in 1972.

But for all of this growth in sales, earnings, stores and shares, Food Town's original shareholders, myself included, really had nothing to show for our success. We had wealth on paper, not the kind you fold into your wallet. Food Town wasn't paying dividends — we needed the money to keep growing — so how could we reward our investors, especially those who had faithfully stuck with Food Town since 1957?

I never thought that folks from Belgium would answer that question.

In the late summer of 1974, I received a letter from a Boston firm specializing in mergers and acquisitions. In essence, it asked whether Food Town would be interested in selling part interest in the company to another firm. I wrote on the bottom of the same letter, "It all depends." I signed my name and drew an arrow at the top. My secretary knew that meant don't waste time typing my response — just Xerox it and send it back to the address at the top of the letter.

About two weeks later, the fellow who wrote the letter called and arranged to visit me in Salisbury. In 1974, the stock market had dropped quite a bit. Food Town was selling for $13 a share at the time. I told the man from Boston I would be interested at $26 a share. I just arbitrarily doubled it. He left and called back in a week's time, saying the firm he was representing — I still had no idea who the company was — would be interested in talking at $25.50 to $26 a share.

"I have no interest," I declared, to the shock of my Boston caller. "I have never mentioned the figure of 25-and-a-half. I have no interest at 25-and-a-half. If you're interested in 26, we'll talk. If not, we won't talk."

He and his client were interested. Finally, we arranged to meet in New York on a Monday. By then, I had learned the interested party was a Belgian firm, Establissement DelHaize Freres et Cie — or Delhaize Le Lion for short. The company was Belgium's second largest grocery chain, whose roots in the business went back 90 years before the start of Food Town. I didn't know it then, but protectionist measures in Belgium stifled supermarkets' potential for growth, forcing Delhaize to look toward the United States for investment purposes. The Belgians had instructed the Boston firm to find a supermarket chain smaller than it was. Settling on the Southeast, the firm presented Delhaize with 10 names, and Food Town was one of them. Eventually, Food Town became the lone finalist, so to speak.

On the Saturday before we were to meet in New York, I received a letter outlining 31 stipulations I could not live with. It was as though we had never talked. I called Boston and told the fellow I wasn't going to New York. He said I had to — the Belgians had already left.

"That's their problem, not mine," I answered. "You sent me 31 things that I'm not going to agree to, and I'm not wasting my time or the company's time going up there."

Frantic, the man in Boston asked whether I would meet them in Charlotte Monday. I agreed, but reminded him I wasn't even going to bring a lawyer because of the 31 things I would never agree to.

The Belgians flew to Charlotte, and we talked. One by one, they conceded to the 31 points. I agreed to fly to New York the next day with Tam Shuford, Food Town's attorney on retainer. In Charlotte, I met Guy Beckers, president of Delhaize; Gui de Vaucleroy, a member of the company's executive committee; and Jacques LeClerq, whose idea it was to invest in America. While there would be some tensions over the years, especially in our initial negotiations, the men became friends and business partners through the years. They spoke perfect English. I recall that in New York, where we met in the uptown law office of White and Case, I tried to make conversation and immediately put my foot in my mouth.

"You have me at a decided disadvantage," I said. "You speak perfect English, and all the French I know is 'Buon giorno.'"

They quickly informed me that I had just said "Good morning" or "Good day" in Italian.

"I spent 25 months in Italy," I laughed. "Now I know what I learned."

In our New York negotiations, as we discussed a 10-year voting agreement, the Belgians insisted on equal board representation. I refused.

"You can have 20, I'll have 21," I said. "You can have three. I'll have four. Whatever number you need, give me one more and that's what's going in the contract."

They finally stood up and said they would have to call Brussels about conceding the point on board representation. In my opinion, they went to the restroom, smoked a cigarette and came back. Anyway, they agreed that Food Town would have one more member on the board. Soon, we came to another roadblock. They wanted Food Town to agree to pay out a third in dividends. No way, I said.

"I'm not going to pay any dividends," I continued. "We don't pay any now. We need it to open new stores."

They kept insisting, and I kept refusing, reminding them of our discussions the day before in Charlotte.

"No problem," I finally said. "I'm sure you did what I did when you came here. I bought a roundtrip ticket. I can go home. I'm sure you can. We've got no problem. We'll just agree to disagree."

If the truth be known, I really wanted our deal to go through, thinking again of how our shareholders would finally receive some return on their faith and loyalty.

"I'll tell you what I'll do," I offered. "I'll agree in the contract to think about it. I'm telling you right now I'm not going to do it. But if it would make you look better and feel better, I will agree to sign an agreement that I'll think about it each year."

The Belgians finally agreed. About 11 p.m., I told them I was going to bed and advised them to do the same. Leave it to Tam Shuford and their attorneys, I said. I forcefully told Mr. Shuford not to concede anything and let me know the next morning if they had worked out a deal. I called him about 9.

"Yes, they finally agreed to it about 4 o'clock," he said. "Every time I turned around, they tried to hide something."

The final agreement went like this: Delhaize would purchase 50,000 shares of stock from Food Town Stores Inc. for $26 a share, or a total of $1.3 million. Delhaize would purchase 68,000 shares from the five Food Town directors at $26 a share, or $1,768,000. (This represented 37 percent of the holdings of each director.) Delhaize would purchase up to 198,000 shares of the common stock at $26 a share in cash for a total of $5,148,000.

For 34.5 percent of the company, Delhaize invested $8,216,000. The Belgians hadn't achieved exactly what they wanted. They left Brussels intending to acquire 51 percent of the stock, having equal board representation and buying into a company that would pay dividends. But over the years, they eventually reached those goals.

Just about everybody agreed to sell a third of his stock. I wrote a letter to shareholders advising them of my intentions. A shareholder didn't have to sell. I couldn't obligate him or her.

A funny thing happened to Archie Rufty, who some years earlier had resigned from our board, though I'm sure he doesn't consider it too funny. On a Friday, he sold some Food Lion shares at $13 a share. On the following Monday, news of the Belgian deal came out, and shares he had sold for $13 apiece were suddenly worth $26

"My gosh," he said, "why didn't you let me know?"

"You know I can't tell you anything like that," I said. "Why didn't you let me know you were selling it?"

"I didn't want to hurt your feelings," he said.

The Belgian deal meant shareholders would finally see a return on their investment. And Food Town received more cash to help in its expansion.

In 1976, Food Town stock split three-for-one. Sales by year's end were $173 million in 45 stores. Earnings had reached more than $4.8 million. Delhaize had to feel comfortable with its investment, and I quickly learned how comfortable. A stockbroker called me one day and asked whether I knew Delhaize was buying up large chunks of our stock on the open market.

"The hell you say," I answered.

I called Guy Beckers in Brussels who reminded me nothing existed in our agreement to prevent the Belgians from buying more stock. He explained that Delhaize had to have 50 percent of Food Town's voting stock. Otherwise, the company could not report Food Town's earnings as part of their earnings in Belgium. That makes sense. Our earnings were more than their earnings, and I knew from the start they would eventually try to gain a 50 percent interest in Food Town.

"But if you're going to do it," I told Guy, "I think you owe it to my shareholders to offer to buy theirs, rather than buy it from institutions or whoever may have gotten into the market over the years. Give them the opportunity."

So we lined up another meeting at White and Case's office in New York. The stock was selling for $22 a share, and I'm trying to get them to think $25. It had split three-for-one, so they'd be paying $75 for something they paid $26 for only two years earlier.

"Mr. Ketner," a White and Case attorney said, "you don't understand. They don't need your permission to buy this stock."

"I understand that," I said. "I'm sure they understand that I understand. The thing that you probably don't understand is if they don't do it the way I want to, it's going to make me mad as hell. And I don't think their intent is to make me mad as hell."

Delhaize agreed to buy at $25 a share.

Part of the agreement was that I couldn't sell any of my stock, because the Belgians didn't want me to lose interest in moving the company forward. As it turned out, they did me a favor. I have a lot more stock today than I would have by selling then. To attain its desired percentage of 50 percent and a fraction, Delhaize purchased 391,000 shares, adding to its existing 1,027,000. The Belgian interests also would purchase 50,000 shares of stock from Food Town. The Belgians' second big investment in Food Town amounted to $11,025,000, meaning they had more than a $19 million interest in the company.

I did my best to reassure people that the Belgians' having controlling interest in the stock did not mean they would be managing the company. The voting agreement made sure of that. It called for 80 percent of the board to approve any changes at Food Town, and more than 50 percent of the board had to be Food Town people.

The first 10 years covered by our voting agreement ran out quickly. Of course, each time a voting agreement comes up for renewal, the Belgians demand certain things. My biggest fault is that I can see the other person's point of view. Their stock had gone up in value tremendously in Belgium, just as ours had here. The Belgians came to me one day and said Food Town had to do something about paying them dividends. In Belgium, companies paying low dividends carry a stigma, especially if they're the lowest-paying on the market. And Delhaize was. Another dilemma: Two brothers started the company 125 years ago, so there were fourth and fifth cousins — everybody in the business — relying on their dividends to live. So I could see their problem but, at that time, I wasn't willing to concede a very large dividend. To me, the better stocks in the United States don't pay dividends because they're growth stocks.

I asked them why they didn't sell part of their stock. They couldn't because selling would leave them with less than 50 percent of the stock. Then I suggested that we make the next stock split a two-for-one but give an equal amount in non-voting stock. Food Town could have two classes of stock, A and B, letting the B stock be the voting stock. I suggested to the Belgians that they keep their B stock but sell some of their A shares to raise the money to pay for their dividends.

That's what happened, and that's why Food Lion has two classes of stock today. I think the Belgians sold $30 million worth of A stock. When you think about it, Delhaize invested a total of about $19 million in 1974 and 1976. It sold stock for $30 million. So they have a minus $11 million investment and have received dividends amounting to millions of dollars.

Delhaize and Food Town/Food Lion have had an interesting relationship through the years. As part of the first deal, Delhaize sent a controller over to watch our books.

"You pay his salary," I said, "because I'm not going to pay his salary or anything because we don't need him. But I don't blame you. I would send somebody over here to check up on these foreigners."

"The fellow who came — one of the cousins — could hardly speak English. And we spoke no French, so it was a waste of time. I kept saying we ought to send him back. I didn't mind his being at Food Town. He wasn't irritating anybody. The Belgians wanted to know why I wanted him to go home.

"I say two and two is four and he says 'yes,'" I noted.

"So what's the problem," one of the Belgians asked.

"I say two and two is eight, and he says 'yes,'" I said.

He left soon after. Another time, the Belgians suggested that Food Town's top men take French courses at Catawba College, so that we could converse better with their people.

I gave this response: "Let me explain to you that when my top people know 100 percent of everything there is to know about the grocery industry, then and only then will I consider letting them spend time learning to speak French. And I can assure you now that time will never come. In the meantime, I suggest your people concentrate on learning to speak English because ours are not going to learn to speak French."

I had one week of French in high school and hated it. Miss Emma Marston was probably glad to see me leave.

On a visit to Salisbury after buying into Food Town, the Belgians saw the warehouse being built on Harrison Road. I didn't withhold the information from them. It just didn't enter my mind that it was any of their business. But they asked why I hadn't contacted them about it.

"Why?" I said. "We need it. It's a good price. I bought it."

Delhaize asked to be informed the next time about certain matters, so it wouldn't be a surprise. I said I'd drop Delhaize a note and tell their officials what I had done. I wouldn't be thinking about doing it, I added. It would already have been accomplished.

Early on, the Belgians asked me how many times Food Town had board meetings. They were shocked to hear my answer: once a year.

"There isn't any reason to meet more often than that," I said. "All of us meet — Tom Smith, Bill and I — every Monday morning, so really we have 52 meetings a year. It depends on what you call a board meeting."

My Belgian friends said we had to have more meetings, so I told them to come over every Monday.

"We're not going to pay your air fare if you come," I said. "Let's make that clear. If you come, you pay your own way coming and going because we don't care if you come or not."

I was kind of hard to get along with. We later agreed to quarterly meetings.

One day, a Belgian visitor asked me, "What's your warehouse turnover?" Everybody operates on turnover, and it's suicide to say you don't know. That's ignorance. But I said, "I don't know, and I don't care."

The answer shook them up. They asked how I could say that, when it was the key for pretty much the whole business of selling groceries. They had been in the grocery business all of their lives and knowing the warehouse turnover was an essential.

"It's for everybody else, not me," I said. "I don't believe in it. Turnover has no meaning on the way I buy. If I get a deal of one free for ten, then I'm going to buy extra. So it distorts my turnover. If I've got enough deals in that warehouse, there's no realistic meaning to what turnovers are."

Our conversation took place when interest rates were about 14 percent. One of the Belgians said, "Ralph, one free with ten is 10 percent. You got to pay 14 percent. Explain how that works out."

"For your information," I said, "One free with 10 is nine and one-eleventh percent, if you want to get technical. One of 10 is 10 percent. But let's assume you're right and I buy an extra six-week supply to offer to the customer, which plays havoc with my turn because I've got all this surplus stock out there. Let's suppose I do it and I make 10 percent for six weeks. Six will go into 52 weeks of the year eight and two-thirds times. So if I make eight and two-thirds times 10, I make 86 and two-thirds percent. Now tell me again why I can't afford to pay 14 percent."

They had been in the grocery business 100 and some years, and it never entered their minds that you have to equate movement over a certain period of time, divided by the number of weeks in a year. And the competition never did it, either. Now they're doing it, because it's called forward buying.

I'm not sure how many of Food Town's ideas, such as forward buying, the Belgians have put to use in their own operation. At one time, they were going to try the low-price concept, but they have a unique situation over there. Many times, Delhaize can't open but one store a year and even that hinges on government approval. Also, they have a strong union that has prevented Delhaize from being open on Saturday afternoons or Sundays. On the low-price concept, they finally decided they couldn't increase their volume enough to make it worthwhile. Forward buying at the warehouse level? I would like to think they instituted that. But overall, I just never paid much attention to their operation.

The Delhaize folks came to me one day and said they were going to buy the Alterman's chain in Atlanta, Ga. They asked me what I thought about the deal — they expected to offer $32 million for the unionized chain. If Alterman's offered to give it to me, the answer wouldn't be "no," I said.

"It would be hell, no."

Delhaize had made so much money off Food Lion, I believe they thought this American grocery business was easy.

"I'll tell you two things," I said. "If you buy it, never will I permit any of those people to come up here to see how we operate. And never will I let any of our people go down there. If you make the decision to buy it, you're on your own."

Delhaize bought it. I went down with them one day and walked through the warehouse. Son of a gun, their workers would lift up their feet to take steps, and it seemed like an eternity before their feet would hit the floor again. I told Jacques

LeClerq, "These people are underpaid, these union people. Have you noticed how they hold their feet up in the air? That's hard to do. They should make more money. It's hard work to go that slow."

Delhaize lost its shirt on the operation, eventually selling it.

Delhaize's symbol — the lion — has become a part of the company's name, of course. It also serves as the identifying symbol for our stores and Food Lion's own brands of groceries. Today, Food Lion's board has an equal number of American and European directors — five and five. It's not that big of a deal now, because Delhaize knows the good job Food Lion is doing. Food Lion pays dividends now. And Delhaize maintains a controlling interest in the Class B stock. Each time a voting agreement is renewed, we give a little bit. Overall our partnership has worked out well, despite my confusing Italian for French those many years ago.

9. Buying Low, Selling Low

I was playing bridge one night at the home of John Hartlege, an architect in Salisbury, when he served some instant coffee.

I picked up the jar and looked at the price.

"John," I said, "I didn't know you were a wealthy man."

"I'm not wealthy," he said. "What makes you say a thing like that?"

All the bridge players stopped to listen. "You don't trade at Food Town. That proves you've got plenty of money."

"How do you know I don't trade at Food Town?" he asked.

"You paid 60 cents more for this jar of coffee than we sell it for. I can look at anything in your pantry and tell if you traded with us. I know the price of every item we sell because I set all the prices."

John had to admit that he didn't shop at Food Town, but I think we saw him shortly thereafter.

One minute it seemed like Food Town's new concept — LFPINC (Lowest Food Prices in North Carolina) — was catching on with nearly everybody and the next I'd run into a John Hartlege. Could it be that some people don't want to save money on groceries? We had tried and failed at every gimmick known to man in our first 10 years of business. We just wanted people to like us so much that they would trade with us. That didn't work. We still emphasize being friendly to our customers but we give them something more: the lowest prices in the country.

I was sitting with a bunch of grocery store owners at a food dealers convention, and one of my competitors said he was getting tired of my claiming to have the lowest prices.

"You know," he said, "everybody has about the same prices."

"I'll buy that," I said. "Everybody except Food Town."

"Oh. My prices are as low as yours."

"OK, I'll tell you what you do. You hire a CPA and let him check 5,000 items at your store, the same 5,000 at my store and the one that has the lowest prices takes the other's store lock, stock and barrel."

"Oh, hell no, I won't do that," he stammered.

"You answered my question," I said.

And everybody died laughing. Baxter Shelton, a food dealer from Kannapolis, said, "If you're not up against Food Town, you'd better thank the Lord. I am, and they've got the lowest prices, and don't you ever forget it, either."

Word of mouth is the best advertising in the world, but we had to find a way to sell our concept. Advertising a special price on a can of beans is easy, but it takes a while for people to grasp something like LFPINC. We decided to use television and — to my horror — I let myself get talked into being the spokesman.

Those television commercials were the things I hated above everything else. I'd do 15 takes, and the producer would say, "That's pretty good, Mr. Ketner. Now let's get one more."

One day I just blew up.

"Now listen," I said. "When I left this morning I was president of this company and unless somebody fired me this morning, I'm still president. You can use one of those first 15 takes or just forget the whole thing."

I struggled through the early going with the commercials and thought I was getting better before I ran into a lady in a Food Town store.

Ralph Ketner films a television commercial. "God, I hated them," he said of the taping sessions. "I'd rather work a week than do one." *Photo courtesy of Food Lion.*

"Why, you're Ralph Ketner, aren't you?" she asked. "I recognize you from your commercials."

"Yes, I am," I said, swelling with pride.

"I know you're telling the truth about having the lowest prices."

"Why, thank you, ma'am. I appreciate that."

"Anybody who looks as bad as you do on television just has to be telling the truth."

"Lady," I said. "you sure know how to lift somebody up and knock them back down."

One day I was scheduled to make a commercial about our meat, a subject about which I knew little. It was set up for me to use cue cards, but on the way to Charlotte to film the TV spot, I thought of an entirely new idea. I finalized it during the drive.

The cue cards were up, and the cameras started rolling when I just started talking. "Many of you watching this commercial do not shop at Food Town. Why? Is it because you don't want to save money or because you don't believe me? Either way, I'll make you this offer. If you shop Food Town and spend $15 or more and don't feel you saved money, send me your cash register tape, name and address and I'll send you my personal check for $3. You can't lose."

I almost made it through in one take, but the stunned looks on the faces of the crew got me tickled and about halfway I burst out laughing. They thought I had gone crazy. But I meant what I said.

I set up a special account to send the $3 checks out and began working on a form letter saying, "Enclosed is my $3. . ." Then I realized that just because these people are wrong, I didn't need to give them $3. I changed the letter, starting off with the fact that they were entitled to my $3. But I owe it to you to tell you some of the comments from our customers. "You have the lowest prices I've ever seen," one said. I included about five customer responses and quoted the North Carolina Food Dealers'

Association which made a weekly survey and found we were lower on 97 percent of the 300 items checked.

"In view of the above," I wrote, "I feel that you *owe it to yourself* to give us another try. Enclosed is my gift certificate for $4. Now if you still want your $3 back, send me my $4 gift certificate and I'll give you your $3."

Very, very few ever asked for the $3 check.

Years later, Tom Smith, who was to become the next company president, and I were coming back from Virginia and stopped in a Winn-Dixie in Mount Airy to check it out. A lady recognized me from my television commercials and asked what I was doing in a Winn-Dixie.

"Lady," I answered, "the question is 'What are you doing in here?' "

You see surveys on why people shop where they do. I think they rate, in order, cleanliness, friendliness, courtesy, convenience with price always about fifth. Well that's for the birds because they don't ask an intelligent question: How much price? Can I save a dollar on $10 or do I save a penny? Nine dollars and 99 cents is better than $10 but $9 is a whole lot better. So if you ask the question, I say ask an intelligent question.

Before Ford built the Edsel, it did a lot of surveys. The surveyors asked people what they wanted in a new car. They should have asked what they thought their neighbors wanted, because people really wanted more economy but were ashamed to say so.

There's a story about asking the right question that I like to use.

Back in the old days, the railroad didn't have flashing red lights and arms that come down at the crossings. At night, they had a watchman out there who waved a lantern to let you know a train was coming so you'd stop. Well, there was a terrible wreck and six people were killed at midnight. The family sued and the trial went on for weeks. Testimony revolved around whether the night watchman was telling the truth about having waved the lantern.

The jury found that the railroad was not negligent and didn't award the family any money. The attorney for the railroad said, "Sam, you've saved the railroad millions of dollars, but now it's over. You can tell us the truth about the lantern. You were lying, weren't you?"

"No sir, no sir," the watchman said. "I swore to tell the truth. I wouldn't lie under oath under any condition."

"But Sam, every time they'd ask you a question, you would break out in a cold sweat and start shaking. Why?"

"I was afraid they were going to ask me whether *I lit that lantern*," Sam said.

I got letters from people all the time, challenging me about our prices or asking for a favor. A friend with a new granddaughter called one day wanting to buy some baby food wholesale. I said I'd be delighted to sell it wholesale. Of course, we'd have to raise the price from what it is in the store. We sell baby food at 15 percent below cost.

A woman from Albemarle wrote that a cashier had made her angry. A bag boy had bagged her groceries wrong. She reported it to the manager, and he had made her mad. My stomach was getting tighter and tighter as I read, and I flipped to the second page wondering what was coming next. "Mr. Ketner, I wish I could afford not to trade with you." I loved it. I didn't want to keep buying the customers' business over and over with weekend specials. Now I was "earning it."

Another lady moved from Charlotte to Forest City, and she wrote: "I went shopping today and spent $16 more for groceries than I would have if there had been a Food Town here. What right do you have not to have a Food Town in Forest City?"

I would have loved for her to sue us. Can you imagine the publicity on that?

I talked to another person who didn't believe we had the lowest prices and I offered him this deal: Go anywhere you want and shop, then go to a Food Town. If you don't save at least $6, I'll send you my personal check for $6. In a couple of weeks he called. "Mr. Ketner, I'm the so-and-so who talked to you two weeks ago about saving at least $6. I went shopping with you, and I didn't save $6."

"Well," I said, "I don't see how, but give me your address. . .

"Let me finish," he said. "I bought $100 worth of groceries and I saved $16. I just wanted to tell you how much I appreciated your convincing me to make this test. I wouldn't have believed it."

I hardly believed $16 myself, but the man said he had a couple of dogs and a couple of cats, and the items he started naming were the items we sell at carload cost or less.

A tornado destroyed our store in Bennettsville, South Carolina, and an attorney there called me and said in less than a week the other grocery stores raised prices. They don't have low prices for their customers. They have them for Food Lion. The funny thing is that the Bennettsville store was a terrible location. It had taken years to get to the break-even point. If that tornado had come along five years earlier, it would have saved us a tremendous amount of money.

The past president of Harris Teeter was quoted as saying they have 21 different zoned prices. He didn't say it then, but he meant that the price they charged depended on how close their store was to a Food Lion.

I always had faith in LFPINC, but its power fooled even me occasionally and made me work harder to make it available to everyone. One of those instances came in Monroe where we leased a store from Jim Garrison, a state senator. I had told him that if he had A&P on one corner and Winn-Dixie, Colonial and Kroger on the other three, I would like to have a store dead in the center of those four. The people were already coming there and since we've got the best prices people would trade with us. We leased a store from Garrison in Monroe and part of the lease stated that the developer would not sublease to another competitor. The store manager in Monroe called one day to say that Winn-Dixie was coming to our shopping center.

I called Jim Garrison.

"Aren't you the one who said he wanted to be in the middle of A&P, Winn-Dixie, Colonial and Kroger?" he asked.

"Certainly," I said, "but you've never heard me say I wanted four to build around me. That's what you're trying to do. It's different if I voluntarily come in there, but if you build around me, I'm going to sue."

"You can't sue," he said, "unless you can prove damages."

"Well, we'll just wait and see what happens."

When the Winn-Dixie opened, our sales went up 20 percent. My theory was that they closed a Winn-Dixie to open within half a block of Food Town. Once people drove all the way over here, they figured they might as well drive another half a block and save money."

I didn't get to sue Jim Garrison after all.

The North Carolina Milk Commission wanted to sue me once for selling milk too cheaply. The Milk Commission said I was violating the law by selling milk below a reasonable price. I was selling it at cost. The law read that you have to have at least seven percent markup to cover the cost of doing business. I wanted to be sued because I had already drawn up an ad in my mind. I would have a pair of handcuffs on like I was being led away to prison, saying "The Milk Commission finds me guilty of selling milk to you below what they think I should charge you. If you agree with the Milk Commission, go ahead and let me go to jail. If you agree with me that I should have the right to sell milk at any price I want, then write your representative."

I made the mistake of telling the guy how I was going to beat them in court. "Your law is illegal," I said. "Your law reads that I cannot sell it below the cost of doing business. The average cost of doing business is 18 percent. Now if you find me anybody in the United States who can operate a dairy department — the most expensive part of a store — at seven percent, I'll go to jail. But it can't be done. The law is illegal."

To my regret they decided not to arrest me.

People used to ask me what was the difference between Food Lion and the competition.

"Low price," I would usually say. But said another way, the competition sees how high they can sell something and still sell it. We see how low we can sell it and still make a profit. Two different ideas completely. Our low prices are for our customers. Our competition's low prices are because of Food Lion. And they've acknowledged it. "Look out, Food Lion, we're meeting your prices."

But we couldn't be the low-price leader without efficiency. And without that efficiency we'd have never survived the first 10 years. Food Lion doesn't go in for frills. Nobody flies first class. I didn't, so nobody else did. It might cost $60 more to fly first class. You can walk six feet back and save $60, which is the profit on $6,000 at one percent, which was the industry average at the time. It's much easier to walk six feet.

Nothing is allowed for decorating the offices. While we were over on Julian Road, my office had linoleum on the floor. One day a stockbroker came in and looked around. Ads were stuck up here and there.

"You don't believe in spending any money for decor, do you?" she asked.

"It never entered my mind," I said. "Would sales and earnings be up if we had better decor? Could you sell the stock for more than it's selling for now?"

"You made your point," she said.

We were one of the first in the nation to bale cardboard. Everybody else burned it. There's a tremendous cost, plus you had the environmental people coming around all the time. We started baling it, and instead of spending millions of dollars, we were saving millions of dollars.

We found a thousand ways to cut costs and save time, and one that I used to include in my civic club speeches was about the 35-cent ball-point pens we use. I illustrated the point by pulling out one of the pens and clicking the end. We not only save money on the cost of the pens but we also save a tremendous amount of money in time, as the person using one only had to punch the top of the pen to put it into position to use, whereas if you had something fancy, like a Cross pen, you had to use both hands, as it required a twisting motion to activate it. Remember I said that I used to tell this story. Imagine my embarrassment when the honorarium I received one day as a speaker was, yes, you guessed it, a Cross pen. I immediately removed that story from all future speeches.

We were the first in the industry with what today is called EDLP: everyday low prices. In 1968, we called it LFPINC. We were the first in the country, and probably still the only ones, with centralized buying. Under the old systems, Winn-Dixie, for instance, had buyers at each warehouse. A&P had buyers. Kroger did. Everybody did. But our system, from Day 1, was to have only one set of buyers and that's here in Salisbury. They do the buying for the entire 14 states in which we operate.

We do a tremendous amount of forward buying. That means if there's a deal offered, our buyers are told to buy an extra supply so we can offer it to customers longer. Everybody else is offered the same deal, but their warehouses at that time were not large enough to pull in too much extra merchandise.

Years ago — you'd find better examples now — we bought 19 carloads of quart-size Del Monte ketchup. One item. Nineteen carloads. If you do that, you've got to have larger warehouses.

We have always tried to buy with the customer in mind. Sometimes, it was risky. But if you offered value and low price, you seldom went wrong. I was playing poker with Jim West, head of Bamby Bakery in Salisbury, and I asked how much he charged us for a dozen doughnuts. I think he said 62 cents, and we sold them for 79 cents.

"Jim," I asked, "what does a dozen doughnuts weigh?"

"I don't know exactly," he said.

"For your information, they weigh a pound. I've checked them. You've got flour in there that may cost 10 cents a pound. You've got shortening in there that doesn't cost over 20 cents a pound. There's not a thing in there that costs over 20 cents a pound except the flavoring. It can't cost you over 20 cents a dozen to make them. Your boxes cost so much. Why don't you sell them to me for 30 cents. I'll cut the price to 39 cents, and we'll move them by the truckload?"

"We can't do that," Jim said.

"Call headquarters," I told him, "and tell them that I'll take 30,000 dozen doughnuts which would be a truckload. I'll guarantee the sale. Any we don't sell, I'll eat."

He called. They turned him down.

"You didn't explain it," I said. "Call them back and explain it to them better."

They finally agreed at either 31 or 32 cents. "We've got 30,000 dozen doughnuts coming in Thursday," I told vice president Lawson Saul. "They'll be in the stores on Friday. If any are left over Saturday night, you pay for them. We're selling them for 39 cents instead of 79 cents, and any fool can do that. What I would do, if I were you, would be to tell the supervisors that if any are left, they have to pay for them. They can tell the store managers that if any are left, they have to pay for them. Now that's as far down as it can go, but I'm holding you responsible. At 8:15 Saturday morning, you call me and tell me what the status is so I'll know what's going on."

It was 8:20, and Lawson hadn't called. I called him. "Lawson," I said, "it's 8:20. You were supposed to call me by 8:15. What happened?"

"For your information," he said. "All the damn doughnuts are gone."

"OK," I said, "all is forgiven."

I think we got up to where we sold 90,000 dozen a week. It was a wonderful deal.

We saved our customers a lot of money on health and beauty aids with another innovative idea. We were buying from a distributor and our sales were running approximately $5 million a year. I made the decision to start buying all of the items through our warehouse operation, eliminating the distributor. We did not have sophisticated records at the time, so it was impossible for me to determine exactly what percentage to cut and what percentage of increase it would require to offset this reduction, but in typical fashion, I made the decision that we certainly could operate 15 percent more economically than our distributor. Therefore, I cut every item, approximately 1,000, by 15 percent at the least. This is taking off $750,000 from sales and $750,000 from the bottom line if we could not increase our sales and operate much more economically than our distributor. Quite frankly, I was never able to pinpoint exactly how this decision on my part worked out. I do know that, for the year, our sales were up and our profits were up. Therefore, in my opinion, the decision was a good one as it resulted in saving our customers a minimum of $750,000 while at the same time making Food Town a much stronger competitor.

Some time later, I was invited to appear on a talk show in Charleston, S.C. When you agree to something of this nature, you know that the competition is going to be "gunning" for you. I always play the devil's advocate before appearing on a talk show, whether it be radio or television, trying to anticipate questions that my competitors might ask hoping to embarrass me.

At this particular show, a question did come in, and I feel certain that it was from a competitor. The caller stated, "Mr. Ketner, you keep saying you have the lowest food prices, but aren't you prohibited by law from stating that you have the lowest prices and are limited to saying that you have low prices or lower prices?" I laughed, and I said, "You must be a competitor to ask this particular question. You are correct in that the attorney general from Virginia has written me stating that we cannot use the statement that we have the lowest prices. They have no objection to our saying that we have low prices or that we have lower prices, but we cannot say the lowest prices."

I explained to the caller that I could probably fight the case and win same, as, to the average person, there was little, if any, difference between low, lower, and lowest, but rather than spend $100,000 to $200,000 in legal fees, it was my decision to concede the point and not make an issue of it, thus saving Food Lion all of this money, most of which would ultimately have to be passed on to the consumer. I closed with the statement that I, frankly, did not know the difference between low, lower and lowest, but I did know that Food Lion had low prices, we had lower prices, and we had the lowest prices.

Incidentally, this particular tape from my appearance in Charleston, S.C., was the one that Robin Leach's department apparently bought and cut out segments to make it appear that I had been interviewed for his program "Lifestyles of the Rich and Famous."

I ran up against Virginia state law again with an idea to save every customer money in 1980. At that time we were doing approximately $10 million per week in sales. Every item we had in the grocery department had already been cut, therefore, I saw little advantage in cutting deeper. One morning it came to me that there is one item that costs every shopper who shops at any supermarket: sales tax. I made the decision then to voluntarily pay 1 percent of the 4 percent tax in our stores in North Carolina, South Carolina and Virginia. Now, this 1 percent of $10 million per week is $100,000 per week or $5.2 million annually that I took off the bottom line just by that one decision. It was by no stretch of the imagination, a gimmick or anything of that nature. It was just a judgment decision on my part that if we could save the customers 25 percent on sales tax, then we would be even more entitled to their support and their patronage.

I did not discuss the idea with Tam Shuford, an attorney who was on retainer with Food Town at the time, as it has always been my policy to do what I think is right and then if it develops that I have made a mistake, then get an attorney to help me straighten things out. This proved to be the case in this instance, as the State of Virginia says that you must charge the customer 4 percent and that was it. I put up signs in all our Virginia stores stating, "Virginia state law demands that Food Town charge you 4 percent sales tax. Food Town must abide by the Virginia state laws." I signed it Ralph W. Ketner, President.

We did run it for about a week before we were forced to discontinue it. The State of North Carolina says, in effect, you can do it, but you can't tell anyone. That normally is the kiss of death, but I found what proved to be a way around the law. That resulted in my putting signs in all North Carolina Food Town stores reading, "Rufus Edmisten, North Carolina Attorney General, says that Food Town can charge you only 3 percent sales tax, but they can't tell you that is what they are doing." This was signed Ralph W. Ketner, President. The state of South Carolina says, we don't care what you do, just as long as you pay us the full 4 percent. We continued the reduction from 4 percent to 3 percent for 19 weeks in North and South Carolina, but discontinued it because of the complaints we were getting from our Virginia customers. As I said earlier, it was not a gimmick — it was a way to increase sales as I felt certain that we could increases sales by 10 percent through this promotion, and if you increase sales 10 percent, generally, you can take 1 percent off the bottom line and break even. I have always felt that I would rather have *five fast pennies than one slow nickel*, and this is another example of my thinking and Food Town's philosophy.

In the early '80s, our suppliers and manufacturers started heavily using coupons worth 7 cents, 10 cents, 15 cents, etc. The coupons were issued and redeemable on specific products, just as is done now. Today, coupons generally run for 50 cents to 75 cents whereas back in the early '80s, most of them were either 7 cents or 10 cents. Most of the time the customer would have her order registered before she would look in her pocketbook to determine whether she had coupons. This would have resulted in our having to unbag the groceries to determine whether our customer had purchased a package of Post Toasties or whatever the coupon called for. We made little attempt to police the use of these coupons to the Nth degree, relying upon the honesty of the customer.

I felt certain that our competitors did the same thing, but one day, one of our major suppliers came by my office to see me and stated that his company had hired three ladies who went into three different stores of ours and in each case the cashier had accepted a coupon from the customer without her having purchased the item. I explained to him our policy of not making a big issue of whether or not the customer had purchased the item, as we did not want to go to the trouble of unpacking the groceries to verify same, especially since it was their promotion and not a promotion of ours. He then explained to me that in the future they would not honor any coupons from Food Town and that we would not be reimbursed for the ones now being processed. I explained that he had the right to change the rules in the future, but on all coupons presented thus far, we certainly would expect and demand 100 percent payment. I further explained to him that, if my memory was correct, on the reverse side of all coupons were words to the effect that "the retailer must prove proof of purchase of sufficient quantities of merchandise to justify the coupons presented." I explained to him that we probably bought 20 cases for every one package for which a coupon was presented and that under these conditions he certainly had no claim against Food Town. He didn't buy this argument at all.

I then explained to him that I believe the reverse side of the coupon read, "Any mis-redemption of this coupon constitutes fraud." He readily agreed with me that was true. I said, "In that case, I am going to demand the names and addresses of the three women in question, as I plan to take out a warrant for their arrests as they did fraudulently redeem the coupons at my store and they, in effect, did entrap my cashier." I further explained that immediately I wanted him to start writing their names and addresses. I, in the meantime, would call the sheriff to make certain that the warrants were served properly and promptly. I then looked up the sheriff's number in the telephone directory knowing all the time that I was going to call my house were no one was home. This I did, but, in the meantime, while the telephone was ringing supposedly in the sheriff's department, he is urging me to hang up and let him think about the matter and discuss it. I reluctantly agreed to do so, thus ending, I thought, the problem with that particular company on coupon redemptions.

I was wrong. About two months later this representative called and stated that he and four of the other top officials with his company wanted to talk to me about coupon redemption. I explained to him that I thought we had handled that before. He said no, it was necessary that they talk to me again. So, I set up an appointment, probably a couple of weeks later, and five representatives showed up for the meeting. It was in my office on Harrison Road. The representative that I had the trouble with some months before introduced the other four people, one of whom was the Southeastern Sales Manager. The other three were vice presidents from various departments, legal, etc. Each of them explained to me what their position was with the company beginning with the Southeastern Sales Manager.

I immediately turned to him and said, "I realize that the other four people here outrank you, and, therefore you are not going to be in a position to say too much, but, just out of curiosity, how much are our sales up with you this year compared to a year

165

ago?" I think the figure he said was 60 percent or 75 percent. I said, "I thought that was somewhere in line with our records, but I wanted to hear you say it. These four big shots from headquarters who have nothing to do with sales are here to attempt to kill your sales and, instead of being up 60 to 75 percent, what they do might result in a sales decrease rather than a sales increase, but I want you to know that I understand the awkward position that you are in and the fact that you will not be able to speak up regarding this matter." I then turned to the other four, and I said, "What do you all have in mind?" Their point, which they stuck to from beginning to end, was that the cashier would say to the customer when she started through the checkout stand, "Do you have any coupons?" I explained to them that that would start a monologue because the customer would say, "No, they didn't give me one — where were they?" And then it would go on from there resulting in the customer thinking that she had failed to receive something she should have received. I said that we would not, under any condition, have our cashiers do this because of some few coupons that they felt might be being mis-redeemed. They explained that, if I did not follow their plan, that they would, in the future, refuse to honor any coupons submitted by Food Town.

I said, "I believe you mean that."

They said they did.

I said, "Well, just a minute. I want you to hear a conversation I am going to have with my head buyer." I then called the head buyer for Food Town and explained that I wanted him to cut 50 percent of the items being purchased from that particular company. In other words, if we were buying 40 items, to immediately discontinue 20 and buy the 20 fastest sellers. I also wanted him to cut the facings. In other words, if they had 10 facings on the shelf, reduce that to five so that, in effect, we would show to the customer only 50 percent of the facings being sold at that time. I looked at the Southeastern Sales Manager and asked, "What effect do you think that will have on your sales?" He said, "It will cut our sales approximately 50 percent." I said, "Instead

166

of a 50 to 60 percent increase, you are now going to look at a big decrease. He said, "That is true." I said, "this will result, in my opinion, in probably your division not meeting its quota and, as a result, losing all bonuses, etc." He again agreed that I was correct. I then looked at the four officials from headquarters and said, "Is this what you want?" They said yes. I said, "Okay, there is no point in further discussing the matter. You all leave."

They got to the door and I said, "Wait a minute. If I were your president, and you came back and told me what you just accomplished at Food Town, I would fire all four of you. You don't want that. If he had wanted to send a cut and dried message, he would have sent it by mail or would have called and told me. He sent the four of you here thinking that you had the intelligence to work out some sort of compromise that would be beneficial for all concerned. Instead, you have come with the idea that you would dictate to me what we would have to do. You have already seen that this is not the case, because we have things what we can do, and I guarantee you that they will be done. Your president sent you because he thought he was sending intelligent people to represent him, but so far, you haven't shown this to be the case. Now, let's sit down and think this thing through and see if there is a compromise that we can reach."

We sat there for a little bit, and finally I said, "I'll tell you what let's do. I believe this is the way to handle it. In the future, when the coupon is presented from your company, I will have my cashier ask the customer, 'Did you purchase this item?' Now, we have already established that 98 percent of the coupons are correctly handled, leaving 2 percent subject to mishandling. We both agree, I feel certain, that 90 percent of the people will truthfully answer that question when asked by the cashier. So, this cuts down the margin of error from 2 percent to .2 of 1 percent, meaning that 99.8 percent of all transactions will be correctly handled in the future. Now, this is a compromise that your president would be proud to hear, as it would not necessitate my canceling 50 percent of your product and reducing facings by 50 percent."

They thought for a minute and said, "He won't buy that."

"No," I said, "he won't buy that unless you buy it. Now, first, let me explain to you that this is your idea, not mine, because he is not going to give you any brownie point for my thinking up the solution. You go back to him explaining that you had thought of this idea and had presented it as a matter of recourse after having heard me tell my head buyer what to do."

I finally convinced them that this was the intelligent way to handle the matter. They left pretty well assured that they would be able to sell the president on *their* idea. Three days later, one of the officials called me and said the president thought that was a wonderful idea, and that was the way we handled it from there on in.

To me, these kinds of problems were what made the job so fascinating. I thoroughly enjoyed my work as head of Food Lion because, in every case, I was fighting for the benefit of the customers. As long as you do that, you have a right to succeed.

But reality has a way of making all our problems seem small. There was a nasty rumor going around town one Sunday morning: *I was dead.*

Tam Shuford, my old friend and lawyer, called early that morning, and I answered the phone.

"Ralph," he said, "Is that you? Are you all right?"

"Yes," I answered, "it's me. And I'm all right. Why shouldn't I be?'

"Because there's a rumor going around town that you died last night, and your body's at Summersett's Funeral Home," he said. "I called the hospital and they confirmed your death. I called the funeral home and they confirmed having your body. I can't tell you how relieved I am to hear your voice."

Tam told me to get out of bed, get dressed as quickly as possible and show myself around town. Ruth and I got in the car and set off. We hadn't gone far before a driver passed us going in the opposite direction. Suddenly, his car swerved as he turned to stare at a ghost.

I never found how that rumor got started, but if I had died that Sunday I'd have taken the secrets of LFPINC with me. I knew then it was time to find a successor and start thinking about the future of our little grocery chain.

10. Four-Letter Words

"Several years ago, I had the opportunity to hear an extemporaneous hour-long monologue about the indescribable pleasure to be derived from a lifelong devotion to controlling costs. The speaker was one of the true masters of the art, Ralph Ketner, co-founder of Food Lion Inc., the $7-billion supermarket chain based in Salisbury, N.C. His talk was mesmerizing and energizing.

— George Gendron, editor-in-chief, *INC* magazine

I hear the question in some form or the other all the time: "What's the secret of success?" People who ask that question already have missed the point. There's nothing secret about it.

I can give a simple definition of a successful person: He's someone who is happy with his job and family life. But when people talk about the "secrets" of success, they're looking for an easy way out. They want to be an instant winner. They want to have the lottery's lucky number.

In 1982, Tri-State College in Indiana asked me back as commencement speaker. For that speech, I concentrated on what I believe are the essential elements of success. I came up with a series of four-letter words: home work, hard work, team work, Good Lord, good luck and good idea. Apply these principles and you'll be successful. What's so secretive about that?

In Food Lion's case, for example, the good idea was LFPINC. The good luck was our competitors' failing to catch on and that we had the cost-conscious operation necessary to make it profitable. The Good Lord had to have been with us throughout. I worked plenty of 100-hour weeks, and I know we had some of the best people in the grocery business working together to save people money on their food bills.

Now I believe in planning — home work — but not necessarily in the traditional business fashion. A couple of years after the Belgians had bought an interest in Food Town, one of them said to me, "Ralph, we haven't seen your five-year goals."

"You won't," I told them. "If you get down to a year, you won't see them. You get down to a week, you won't see them. I'm a firm believer if I do the best I can today, I'm going to come out ahead."

Now I'm not saying that next year Food Lion haphazardly adds 100 stores without any kind of planning. But we don't project what each one of those stores is going to do. How could we? A store's location has a lot to do with things. We don't know how the competition will respond. To me, budgeting is for the birds, yet everybody does it. It's an exercise in futility. If I'm a store manager in Salisbury, don't project for me what I'm going to sell in 1993. What if Wal-Mart opens up next to me? Or a new Winn-Dixie? You're going to hold me to that budget projection you worked out last year? Man, you're wasting your time.

Now, if you're going to open 100 stores, you better make sure your finance man has money or knows where he can get it. But as far as trying to figure out what your stores are going to do, that's ridiculous.

In planning, I'd rather have good ideas. I went to a "Phillips 66" brainstorming session once at Hillsdale College. The seminar had nothing to do with the oil company. Don Phillips was president of Hillsdale College at the time.

One of his seniors writing a thesis concluded that 95 percent of the talking done at big meetings of General Motors, General Foods — all the big boys — was done by 5 percent of the people. It was obvious the other 95 percent could contribute something, but they were afraid to stand up and risk making fools of themselves. Phillips wanted to know how to get these people to participate, and he devised a method for brainstorming.

At the seminar, Phillips put six people at each table and gave each group six minutes to thrash out a problem. The answer could not go more than 10 words. Each person received a three-by-five card, and each group elected a spokesman.

The hypothetical problem for each group: How can a company sell more blackboard erasers? (I failed to mention that all of us were supermarket operators, whose closest association with blackboard erasers had been back in school.) In the group, each person thought of his own answer. I remembered having to clean the erasers in school as a form of punishment. I suggested building in obsolescence. Make erasers in layers. When the bottom became all chalked up, just pull off a layer and you have a clean one ready to go.

One guy noted that no one could ever find the chalk. Why not put an attachment on the back of the eraser that would hold a piece of chalk? The group came up with several brilliant ideas — just like that, and the question was cold.

The moderator asked for the six ideas from each table, then instructed each table to put forth its best idea. This all took about 10 minutes. I believe there were about 17 tables — maybe 100 people. A person from each table wrote his group's best idea on the blackboard, so within minutes you have the best thinking of 100 people. It was crucial that the idea be expressed in 10 words or less. And none of the ideas could be criticized, even if you said, "Give a date with Marilyn Monroe with each gross."

This approach just can't be beat in business for attacking problems. I used it a lot of times. I would present the problem and simply ask the team I had with me, "What would you do?" I recommend it highly to any business today. If you have a problem and 10 to 12 people in your group, have them sit down and write out two or three ideas. Don't let them exceed 10 words. I've actually taken the Phillips seminar a step further. After the meeting I would pick up all the three-by-five cards. What they thought was good and chose as the best idea may not be as good as what I could find in the other cards, rework in my mind and make 10 times better. So pick up all the cards. Say we'd have 20 supervisors in for a meeting. At the end, I could pick up 20 cards with three ideas each, and I'd have 60 ideas that I could take home and, in my leisure, choose the ones that I thought would work.

It works outside of business, too. Years ago, Salisbury wanted to become an All-American City. The organizers needed to enlist ideas from citizens on how to improve Salisbury. I told them I had the perfect way. Every civic club in the city devoted one program to the brainstorming technique I learned at the Phillips seminar. If Salisbury had 10 civic clubs with 100 members each, within a hour's time the city had 1,000 ideas on improving the city from some of the leading business people in town. It's great. It worked and Salisbury was chosen an All-America City.

"Hard work" represents four-letter words I became well acquainted with in life and with Food Lion. So did others who worked for the company. In my talks to college business schools, I mention that vice presidents who put in less than 60 hours a week for Food Lion are, in my opinion, considered part-time employees. The MBA candidates in the audience always perk up when I say that. More than once, a student will come up to me afterwards and say, "Mr. Ketner, we enjoyed what you had to say, but you turned us off with all that talk about 60 hours being a short work week."

"I mentioned that for a reason," I say. "I just felt that, in case you've given any thought to working for Food Lion, you'll know what to expect and what we'll expect of you."

I always enjoyed the work and disagree with the psychologist who tried to tell me my 80- and 100-hour work weeks were a sign of insecurity. Insecurity wasn't keeping me on the job. I had a tiger by the tail, and a regular 40-hour work week wasn't going to allow Food Town to grow and prosper the way I realized that it could.

In that regard, a Food Lion executive has to be highly motivated, or he'll be left behind. And with the company's dramatic growth, a motivated employee at any level has the chance for quick advancement. The employees' drive has helped Food Lion succeed. But I think it's important for management to realize that all employees don't want on the fast track.

Ronnie and Donnie Marsh, twin brothers and longtime store managers in Salisbury, are good examples of the importance of leaving employees where they want to be. The Marshes didn't want to be promoted. They loved what they were doing and liked being close to each other and their families. The best thing you can do with competent people like that is leave them alone. Now, I was the type who had to be promoted or I'd quit and go somewhere else.

The Marshes, by the way, retired at age 45, and they could do it because of their enormous amount of money in profit-sharing, all of which was contributed by Food Lion.

In 1963, we set up a profit sharing plan so that, Lord willing, if we were still in business 20 to 25 years down the road, we would be able to give our employees more than a gold watch. We didn't want to wonder if the retiree was going to be able to live well in their remaining years. We started by putting 20 percent of pretaxed earnings into profit-sharing for eligible employees, including cashiers and baggers. The government had a limit of 15 percent of earnings, so our policy was 20 percent pre-taxed if it did not exceed the 15 percent maximum. For the past 29 years, the contribution has been 15 percent of employees' earnings. The employees have never contributed. It's all been put there by the company.

I have always believed in not only working hard, but working smart. Many people start work before they start thinking, and this causes problems. I wanted to illustrate this point to company supervisors years ago. We had just six or eight at the time, and I planned to put in front of each of them two stacks of pennies. One was roughly 80 and the other 20. These two stacks were covered with a paper towel, and I explained to the supervisors at the beginning of the meeting there were 100 pennies underneath. I planned to give a $20 bill to the first person who could tell me how many pennies were in the large stack and would be tempted to fire anyone who counted the big stack. They should count the small stack and subtract that number from 100. Unfortunately, I ran out of time and only had the opportunity to explain the illustration. A supervisor who later became a vice president told me he was glad we didn't actually do the counting. He was sure that he would have counted the big stack.

I did finally get to use the illustration at an accounting class at Mars Hill College years later. I called a volunteer to the front, and he started counting the big stack. I stopped him and asked the class what he was doing wrong. One student said he had used just one hand. No, that wasn't it. Finally, a girl in the back suggested counting the small stack and subtract from 100.

Later on, I told the professor that I'd bet that girl was among the smartest in the class. "She's the smartest," he said. You don't get too many brownie points for working hard unless you work smart, too.

Incidentally, when the young man who began counting the big stack sat down, I said, "Thanks for coming up and thanks for counting the big stack as we had agreed before class and not ruining my point."

A year or two later, I was at a legislative meeting in Raleigh, and one of the state senators came up to me and said: "Mr. Ketner, I want to thank you for what you did for my son at Mars Hill College."

"What do you mean?" I asked.

"My son was the one who went up and counted the pennies," he said "and you kept him from being embarrassed by telling that you two had set it up for him to count the bigger stack, as it would have embarrassed him if you had not protected him as you did."

"I make a point of never trying to embarrass anybody," I said, "because there is enough embarrassment in life without someone deliberately doing it."

More about employees: Good operators, such as Wal-Mart and Food Lion, don't hire nearly as many people to run a store as their competitors.

"We don't create jobs, we create unemployment," I told former Gov. Bob Scott one day.

"What do you mean?" he asked.

"If we can operate a store with 40 people and someone else hires 50, then we use 10 fewer people. But the good side is we save people so much that they'll have money to spend at the hardware store, drugstore and furniture store, and they in turn hire more employees."

So, on the whole, we're hardly hurting the economy.

In a successful business, it's important that the employees never alienate the customer. From the beginning of Food Town, we told the cashiers and store managers to make good on any customer complaints. First, tell the customer you're going to make it good, then ask questions. Don't ask the questions first because it automatically builds up resentment. The customer starts thinking, "He doesn't trust me" or "He doesn't believe me." But after you make it good first, you can ask some questions, and it's easier. You can learn from the customer how the problem occurred and how to keep it from happening again.

Dealing with the customer reminds me of an old grocery store joke. Back in the old days, before the refrigeration stores now have, stores would have to take out the fish and chicken on Saturday nights and place them in 55-gallon cans and ice them down. Around closing one Saturday night, a butcher had only one chicken left. A woman came in and asked for a chicken. He retrieved his lone bird from the can, weighed it and informed her that it was two-and-a-quarter pounds.

"That's perfect, I'll take it," she said.

He started to wrap it up, but the woman said, "You know, I need one a little larger." So he puts the chicken back in the can and draws the same one out, weighs it again and this time tells her it is two-and-three-quarters pounds.

"That's perfect, that's exactly what I need," she says, as the butcher wraps it up and hands it to her.

"You know," the woman says, "on second thought, I believe I'll take both chickens."

I don't know how he got out of that one.

Another joke: Years ago in the produce department, a woman asked for a half head of lettuce. At that time, no one ever cut lettuce into halves. The produce clerk went back to his manager and said, "A stupid lady out there wants a half a head of lettuce. Have you ever heard of such a stupid thing?" He just happened to glance and noticed the same woman standing behind him. It took some fast thinking.

"And this lovely lady wants the other half a head," he said.

Common sense has a lot to do with being successful. One thing I've always believed in: Don't give away your secrets. Remember Robert Stragand, the grocer in Dayton, Ohio, who told me about his low-price strategy? He was very cooperative, and I give him a lot of credit. I went to him time and time again, thanking him for his part in Food Lion's success. But I often wondered why he gave away his secret. You know, Coca-Cola doesn't go to Pepsi and say, "Here's our formula, use it."

So I told my people years ago, "If I ever see your pictures in *Supermarket News* or any other trade publication, I'm assuming you put it out as a resume, and you'll be fired." We love to talk to newspapers and television, so we can tell our story to our customers, but the only people reading trade publications are our competitors and we have no business talking to them. If we were doing something to make us unique or better, I didn't want our competitors reading about it. That's one reason I've argued with Tom Smith about some of his advertisements that show cost-cutting practices aimed at lowering customers' food bills. Our competitors see those ads, too.

Advertising is important to success, and excitement is what advertisement is all about. When Jimmy Carter became president, rice and grits gained in popularity, so I cut the price of rice and grits to cost or below. If a customer realizes she saved 20 cents on grits, she might say to herself, "Thank the Lord for Food Lion. I've saved 20 cents on grits." That's excitement.

Advertising is whatever causes the customers to trade with you. Let me stress again that low prices are the best advertisement in the world. Communicating to the customers about low prices comes next. That's why I hired those two schoolteachers to promote LFPINC years ago.

People measure success in money. Before my brother Glenn sold his stores to Winn-Dixie, my salary was $15,000 a year. For Food Town, I think my salary grew to $30,000 a year by the time we started the Save-Rite warehouse. And Save-Rite was paying me $30,000, but I was giving it all back to Food Town. Before I retired as president and chairman of Food Lion, I think my salary had grown to $225,000 a year, give or take a few thousand.

All I know is, I had fun.

11. Gifts That Keep Giving

I play dirty sometimes — for fun. One day I couldn't help but give the late Dr. Stephen H. Wurster, then president of Catawba College, a nervous moment. Anne and I were meeting with Wurster and the architect who was designing a new, three-story business school building in my honor. We had pledged $3 million toward its construction, so naturally Dr. Wurster kept us updated on the project at every opportunity.

At this meeting, the architect brought out a large, beautiful drawing of the new building, and at the top it said, "Ralph W. Kenter Hall." Note the misspelling of my name. I was the only one to notice the mistake and, without explaining to Anne, I told her to stand up because we were leaving. As we made our move toward the door, the others — Anne, too — wondered what had happened. Was something wrong? Dr. Wurster asked.

I mustered as much sarcasm as I could.

"Since it says on the drawing that Ralph Kenter is paying for this building, I think Ralph Ketner ought to get out of the way so you can invite Mr. Kenter here for this occasion," I said.

If I was going to give $3 million for a building, I at least wanted my name to be spelled right.

You never saw so much apologizing and scrambling to get back into my good graces. The architect explained that a new employee had misspelled my name on the drawing. Well, OK. I soon quit my little game with them. Anne and I returned to our seats, and the project moved past its biggest obstacle — me.

Interestingly, much of the time I've spent reminiscing for this book has been done from my office on the third floor of the Ralph W. Ketner Hall. Yep, it's here, complete with a Tom E. Smith Auditorium. I've been a Catawba College trustee for many years now, and Anne and I have given $7 million to the school through Food Lion stock and other gifts. It also gratifies me to know that much of the funds raised during Catawba College's $28 million capital drive several years back came from money made by Food Lion investors.

Among them was my friend, Zeda Barger. The late Dr. Stephen Wurster, president of Catawba College, asked me if I knew anyone who would be willing to renovate Zartman Dormitory. We visited Zeda and I explained that the college needed to renovate the dorm and if she would contribute $750,000 it would be renamed Barger-Zartman Hall.

"Ralph, I don't have that kind of money," she said. "Jake and I loaned you $500 when you first started Food Town."

"Zeda, you didn't loan me the money," I said. "You bought stock in the company."

"Oh, I knew that," she said. "We knew you needed the money, and we just wanted to help you out."

"Zeda, do you have any idea what that stock is worth today?" I asked her.

"No, not really."

"Well, Zeda it is worth over $3 million. You have a sister, Dot, who is the widow of the founder of Farmers and Merchants Bank. Frankly, Zeda I believe you are as wealthy as Dot.

Zeda couldn't believe it and finally I convinced her that the stock splits over the years— at that time 12,960 for one — had resulted in her being a wealthy person. She gave Catawba College over $700,000 for the dormitory renovations and became a benefactor of Nazareth Children's Home, the town of Faith and many other charities before her death.

Ralph W. Ketner School of Business Building

RALPH W. KETNER HALL
AT
CATAWBA COLLEGE
IS NAMED IN HONOR OF
RALPH W. KETNER
OF
SALISBURY, NORTH CAROLINA
MR. KETNER, A FOUNDER AND CHAIRMAN OF THE BOARD OF
FOOD LION, INC., IS A NATIONALLY KNOWN ENTREPRENEUR AND
INNOVATOR IN THE SUPERMARKET INDUSTRY. HE IS A GENEROUS
BENEFACTOR OF CATAWBA COLLEGE AND HAS SERVED AS A TRUSTEE
OF THE COLLEGE SINCE 1985.

MR. KETNER IS A RARE VISIONARY WHOSE HIGH CHRISTIAN IDEALS,
KEEN BUSINESS ACUMEN, INDOMITABLE SPIRIT, BOYISH SENSE OF
WONDER, DEDICATION TO MANKIND, AND JOYFUL PHILANTHROPY
EXEMPLIFY LEADERSHIP IN EVERY REALM OF LIFE.

DEDICATED ON MAY 3, 1989

The Ralph W. Ketner Hall
located inside the
Ralph W. Ketner School of Business

183

Zeda's sister, Dot, was happy to find out her sister was so well fixed. Over the years, Dot had sent her money on the off chance that she needed it to cover living expenses.

Zeda was like a lot of Food Lion's original investors. They were not educated in the stock market. We paid no dividend for nearly 20 years and after that on an average of less than one percent. Some of the people who owned our stock didn't know what it was worth. When they received a stock split, they just tossed the certificates in a drawer along with the old stock.

People often ask me why I have such an interest in Catawba College. I may be wrong, but I truly believe that the college's students and faculty played a big role in Food Town's early survival — especially that first year. Food Town's first store in 1957 was located about a block from the Catawba College campus. Who knows, but without the students' and faculty's business we may not have made it.

Of course, Food Lion's success has led to wealth for Anne and me that I never anticipated back in those early days. I've always believed that you never really miss money if you give it to people. Or said a better way, *you make a living with what you get but you make a life with what you give.* Catawba College fits in with the approach Anne and I have about much of our giving. Anything involving youth we're partial to — the college, 4-H, Boy Scouts, Girl Scouts, Nazareth Children's Home in Rowan County. These are the kids who are going to grow up and run this country.

Take 4-H, for example. We gave a million dollars toward a new educational wing at the National 4-H Center in Chevy Chase, Md. It was the largest personal gift ever made to the National 4-H Council because I believe in the program. How many kids involved in 4-H end up in prison? I would bet hardly any. As a member of the board of trustees of National 4-H Council, I suggested once that the 4-H fund-raisers find that statistic and use it whenever they call on businessmen for donations.

184

Livingstone College in Salisbury is another organization that I admire. A traditional black college, Livingstone was hit hard a few years ago by Hurricane Hugo. Trees were blown down on property the college owned. I called Dr. Bernard Franklin, college president, and made an appointment to see him. I made him a few offers: a new three-quarter ton truck and a chain saw as well as $125,000 to help with the college's operating fund. I wanted part of the money to be spent to hire college students to cut the fallen trees and deliver it as firewood to needy people. Dr. Franklin accepted my offer, and it was not too long before all of those fallen trees became firewood.

Besides programs involving youth, I've given stock — now worth millions of dollars — to my brothers and sisters, except for Glenn who accumulated his own wealth, but including Brown, who earlier sued me. I've also tried to give gifts when I could to aunts, uncles, all my first cousins on my mother and father's sides and to all my former and current in-laws. And, too, I help a lot of retired ministers by sending them checks.

Linda, my daughter, is heavily involved in working for the homeless in Charleston, South Carolina, so I have contributed a million dollars to her efforts on behalf of HOME (Helping Ourselves Meet Emergencies). Helping the homeless and providing affordable shelter for people has become a major preoccupation of mine, as I'll explain later. I also contributed $1 million to son Robert's alma mater, Duke University. Anne embarrassed me on my 71st birthday in 1991 by paying for a billboard on Innes Street in Salisbury that bore the logos of 10 organizations we had helped out financially. The billboard said, "Thanks, Ralph."

As you might suspect, I get hundreds of requests for donations. One lady wrote me from Nebraska. She wanted $250,000 to renovate a grist mill. She would try to repay me, she said. But if she couldn't, well, I would have renovated a grist mill. I didn't send her the $250,000.

Another lady wrote me and said, "Send me $250,000 so I could do good like you're doing. So I can give it away like you're giving it away." Good try.

Thanks, Ralph!

A surprise billboard for Ralph's 71st birthday.

At long last, a shelter for our homeless and central location for
the many services of Rowan Helping Ministries.

There's something that burns me up about my charitable contributions. Some years ago, the Internal Revenue Service changed the law. A person can donate only 30 percent of his income and get tax credit for it. I still give a lot of money. Right now, I probably have $10 million to carry forward for the next five years. During that five years, based on my income, I will deduct $1.5 million of it. So I've got $8.5 million washed down the drain.

People don't understand that the most tax credit you get is 30 cents on the dollar. You'd still be 70 cents on the dollar better off if you didn't give the money away. So I don't like to hear people say, "Well, it's just a tax write-off for him." It has never been just a write-off for me.

In giving, I've got two things I won't do. One, I won't give to anybody to help pay a doctor's bill. Second, I won't give anything to pay a hospital bill because I'm paying that through increased taxes.

Anne quietly has roped me into many of our charitable pursuits. For two years, a board had been in place whose goal was to build a homeless shelter in Salisbury. But nothing happened. They finally put me on the board. Anne said she wanted to go along with me to my first board meeting, where they were going to elect a new chairman. Later, from the audience, Anne nominated me for the job and the members unanimously agreed.

"Whoa," I said. "Just a minute. She has no right to nominate me. She's not a member of the board."

My protest didn't work, so I had the others explain to me where they were and where they wanted to go. Someone suggested that we appoint a committee to work on getting a shelter.

"No," I said, "if we appoint a committee, it doesn't get done. Anne and I will guarantee it. I'll either pay the money or raise the money."

I explained that I would write 30 of my friends in hopes that 25 of them would agree to contribute $10,000 each and Anne and I would give $250,000 reaching the $500,000 needed. That's what we did, and 25 of them gave their money — as I knew they would. I wrote the other five who I knew wouldn't give any money, just so they would have a chance to turn me down again. Then the next time they came to me for a gift, I could turn them down. The shelter was built, and today volunteers give thousands of hours a year in staffing it. My hat's off to anybody who gives of his time. Giving money is one thing, but giving time deserves a lot of recognition. Anne devotes so much of her time to Nazareth Children's Home.

Years ago, the folks at Nazareth asked me to be on their board. Basically, it was a way of seeking some money. I told them they should ask Anne — she would love to. What an understatement. I joined her on the board a couple of years later, but, boy, the kids love her. Any frequent visitor to our home the past five or six years has probably smelled a cake baking in the oven on at least one occasion. Anne makes a birthday cake for each child. The home used to have one flat cake per month for all the children who had birthdays in that month. Anne wanted to do something nicer for the kids. First, she started out making each child a chocolate cake — her favorite. But it wasn't long before they started calling the house with special requests.

"Mrs. Ketner, could I have one in the shape of a basketball that says, 'To Laura, from Michael Jordan?'" one girl asked. Anne made it. She just delights in the whole thing. All the time, she's throwing parties for the children and traveling the 10 miles or so to visit them. She started having a prom dance for the older kids because many of them often weren't invited to their school's prom.

Each of the children has a story: child abuse, sexual abuse, being burned with cigarettes, malnourished. As you can imagine, it takes a long time for them to come along because they've been mistreated much of their lives. Ernest Huntley is one of our favorites. He calls Anne and me "Mom" and "Dad." He's a big kid who won a school wrestling championship. He should — he weighs about 200 pounds. Anne's mother visited Nazareth one day for the dedication of a building whose renovation we had funded.

"Grandmother, how are you?" the boy shouted.

"You must be Ernest," Anne's mother said. Incidentally, Ernest is African-American.

We've taken the children to a 4-H event in Washington, D.C., the Ice Capades, circuses and stuff like that. I once rode on their school bus with them — never again. Paul Fisher of F & M Bank in Granite Quarry has sponsored a trip for them to Disney World. I sometimes remind the children that they see a lot of things the average kids never see.

Anne pretty much directed the renovation of a campus building which became a Home for Independent Living for Girls, and she designed a new 1,680-square-foot building to serve the same purpose for the older boys. She came up with the idea for independent living: PAL, Preparation for Adult Living. It gives the boys and girls a chance to balance their own checkbooks, cook their own meals, manage their hours, etc. I remember when an architect came back to me with a quotation on what the boys' new building would cost: $350,000. I couldn't believe the high price. He showed me some elaborate plan that included a recreation room.

"Fella," I said, "the whole purpose of this building is to teach these kids how to live after they leave here. Tell me how many of them will make enough money that the place they rent will have a recreation room, exercise room and all this stuff. I want the bare essentials. I want two to three to a room so they learn to live like they'll have to. It's going to be rough when they leave here."

It was built for much less.

My retirement sometimes has felt like one big building project. For two to three years, as Anne and I drove through Salisbury, we would pass the Wallace Building, at seven stories the downtown's highest structure. When I was a kid, I used to sell newspapers at the Wallace Building, where there was a basement barber shop. The barber owed a lot on his grocery bill, so my dad would send me there to get my haircut and take the price off whatever the barber owed him. It embarrassed me. I thought my dad was borrowing from the barber when all along it was the other way around.

Those had been much better days for the Wallace Building, when its first-floor retail spaces were prized locations on the town's square and professionals, including many doctors, filled the upper floors. But vacancy became the main occupant and, from the outside, it looked like the devil. What especially irritated Anne were the cockeyed blinds in many of the windows. She kept saying someone ought to do something about the Wallace Building. Well, I'm a slow learner.

One day I found myself going to David Treme, Salisbury's city manager, and saying Anne and I might have an interest in buying the Wallace Building and rehabilitating it under certain conditions. The city had an option on the building. In an agreement, I said if the bids for renovating the building came in at $2.4 million or less, I would agree to certain things. If the bid came in 10 percent over the $2.4 million, either party had the right to back out. The bid came in at 50 percent more, so it killed everything.

I then changed my formula a little bit at a meeting with Mayor John Wear.

"You're trying to get out of this," he said.

"Whoa, let's back up," I said. "I am out. I believe you're trying to get me back in. When it came in at 50 percent over, you were out and I was out and we are starting all over again."

We reached a new agreement. I agreed to increase my commitment by 10 percent, which I would have had to do had the bid come in at 10 percent over. The other concession had to be on the city's part, but it would still have access to the second floor for offices, and I agreed not to raise the rent, even though it would cost more.

To make a long story short, the city and the Ketners became partners. It's the only thing that could have happened to save the building, for which the owner wanted $300,000. It would have cost that much just to blow it up and haul it away, leaving a hole in the middle of town.

The original intent was for Anne and me to own it. We planned apartments from the third floor up. I wanted affordable, beautiful apartments made available to people such as retired school teachers and retired postal workers, who don't have a lot of money and can't afford to rent these $600 and $700 a month places.

I knew I was going to lose a slug of money. I called my son, Robert, the day after I committed to buying the Wallace Building. Remember, he's a vice president with Merrill Lynch.

"Dad, do you think that's a good investment?" he asked.

"No," I answered. "Don't try to have me committed for being senile. I know what I'm doing. I'm going to lose my shirt. But as long as I do it knowingly, to provide nice accommodations for people who perhaps couldn't afford them, then I'm doing it for a purpose."

After about a year — April of 1991 — I asked Anne a question while we were spending some time at our place in Sarasota, Florida.

"Honey, what would you say if we gave that building to the city? I don't want people calling me saying their faucet leaks or this and that."

Now bear in mind, the Wallace Building would be producing considerable income. The city would be paying about $40,000 a year for the second floor. In all, it would generate $200,000 to $300,000 income a year, but it was still a poor investment for the $2.6 million and all the taxes and insurance. Anne, who had put as much time as I had into seeing the renovation through, left the decision up to me. I called the city with our offer to donate the building. Treme didn't take long with his answer of yes.

THE PLAZA

THIS PLAQUE IS PLACED ON
OCTOBER 18, 1991, IN HONOR AND
RECOGNITION OF ANNE AND RALPH
KETNER FOR THEIR UNPRECEDENTED
GENEROSITY TOWARD THE CITY OF
SALISBURY. AFTER ENTERING INTO
PARTNERSHIP WITH THE CITY TO MAKE
THE PLAZA RENOVATION A REALITY, THE
KETNERS GRACIOUSLY DONATED THE
PLAZA TO THE CITY ON APRIL 9, 1991 AS A
"GIFT FROM THE HEART, TO THE CITY WE
BOTH LOVE."

CITY COUNCIL:
DR. JOHN E. WEAR, MAYOR
MARGARET H. KLUTTZ, MAYOR PRO TEM
R. DARRELL HANCOCK
PAM J. HYLTON COFFIELD
CHARLES L. SOWERS

CITY MANAGER:
DAVID W. TREME

ARCHITECT:
LAMBERT TATE ARCHITECTURE

GENERAL CONTRACTOR:
CABARRUS CONSTRUCTION COMPANY

THE PLAZA

The focal point of Salisbury's beautiful historic downtown, now restored to its turn of the century splendor.

Today, the old skyscraper, renamed The Plaza, looks great inside and out. The upper four floors are apartments, and all have been rented. The second and third floors house offices, and three street-level spots have been leased. The city has placed a higher rent on the apartments than I would have charged, but they're sort of obligated to do that. If the city rented those apartments at $275 to $300 a month, the other property owners in Salisbury would scream bloody murder. The city upped the rent a couple of hundred dollars to what the traffic would bear.

I never learn. The city and I also work closely on an affordable housing program aimed at helping people buy their first homes. It originated from an article I read about four years ago in *Reader's Digest*. The author had returned to Peru where on one side of a river he saw beautiful homes. On the other side of the same river were slums. And both sides had started out being developed by the same tribe. The only difference was that people who owned their homes lived on the nice side. People who rented their houses lived in the slums.

A homeowner has more to offer society than a renter, so that got me thinking. Maybe we could supply financial help and also assemble people to really make houses that were both quality and affordable. We started with one home in Salisbury. I convinced Jake Fisher to sell us one of his modular homes at a low cost. We then used the city staff to screen applicants for low-interest loans and received cooperation from Omnibank in Salisbury to make the money available. In the end, we came up with a $40,000 house requiring a $2,000 down payment. They have 1,088 square feet, three bedrooms and two full baths. Monthly payments are less than $340. By early 1993, we had built 13 homes in Salisbury within 24 months. Truthfully, I'm disappointed. By now, I thought, we could have built 100 homes in Rowan County alone and 1,000 to 10,000 in the nation. I assumed that if this idea worked, it would revolutionize the country.

But we got no help from Washington — handcuffs on everything. I met with Jack Kemp, at that time secretary of Housing and Urban Development, in Greensboro, North Carolina. I explained that I had roughly $1 million that I wanted to make available for affordable homes and asked if his department would meet with me. I did not hear from him in 30 days and wrote one of his aides. Again, I did not get a reply until a Mr. Rosenthal called asking me to come to Washington along with Gayle Peeler and Larry Chilton, who had helped make the program work in Salisbury.

The Salisbury Post carried a headline reading: "Ketner goes to the top: Washington." It should have read: "Ketner goes to the bottom: Washington." Rosenthal told me I was trying to help the wrong people.

"You are trying to help the low income people who have credit problems," he said. "You need to help the more affluent people."

"My gosh," I said, "affluent people don't need help. I am trying to help those people become home owners and better citizens, and you are telling me that there is no way that you can do it."

It later developed that he was telling the truth. Regulations prohibit loaning money unless certain conditions work out to the Nth degree. And I mean the Nth degree. The intent was there, but it just did not work out. I plan to keep trying.

I've had other frustrations with government when I've had good ideas in which I was offering money in exchange for government's chance to be more efficient. I wrote Gov. Jim Martin of North Carolina once to offer the state $20,000 a year — $5,000 for each quarter — payable to the city, county or state employee who turned in the best money-saving idea. Government always thinks first about raising taxes, not cutting expenses. I thought if I offered $20,000 incentive money for ideas, great ideas would come through. I told the governor about the meter

195

readers I had observed in Salisbury. One guy would call out a figure, and the other meter reader would write it down. I called the mayor.

"We've got two men out there reading a meter," I complained. "Why don't you give one of them a dictaphone, read into that, come back and transcribe it. There would be fewer errors, and you'd cut out the cost of half the meter readers."

The city took my advice. The governor expressed interest in my proposal and sent Jim Lofton, the secretary of administration, to see me. I thought we understood each other until I received the agreement papers, which stated that the award was limited to state employees. I didn't want to limit it to state employees, because I'm interested in 100 counties. If I can find one idea in this county that works, then I can multiply it by 99. It would work the same with cities, and there are more than 400 cities and towns in North Carolina.

I suggested to Lofton that we had to include both cities and counties and I've since offered the county and city associations $10,000 each under a similar proposal. The county governments accepted the idea, and it's working. The trouble you have to go through to give away money and entice government to save it!

I report to my new Ketner School of Business office every morning because all these projects, correspondence and speaking engagements keep me busy. That day when I shocked Dr. Wurster by standing up and heading out the door seems like long ago, but it wasn't the last time the building's name would lead to a nervous moment for the college president.

One day I drove into a campus parking lot and noticed a car with the personalized license plate, "RWKSOB." Did that mean what I thought it meant? I saw Wurster a few minutes later.

"If that's what they think of me here at Catawba," I told him, "I'll just have to resign as a trustee and sever all my connections with the college."

Dr. Wurster swallowed hard. He went out with me to see the license plate. Sure enough, there it was. He promptly promised that he would deal harshly with the person displaying the rude and tasteless message. A secretary heard our exchange and immediately started to laugh.

"That license plate belongs to Dr. Erik Oldenberg," she said. "His wife gave it to him for Christmas, and he's very proud of it."

Dr. Oldenberg, you see, teaches at the Ralph W. Ketner (RWK) School of Business (SOB). It led to a good laugh. Poor Dr. Oldenberg never dreamed anyone would read something else into his license plate. He decided, however, to take it off his car and presented it to me as a gift. I keep it in my office, where it means what I want it to mean.

12. Some Family Notes

About 2 a.m., I heard a noise in our getaway home at Litchfield Beach. I'm not the bravest soul in the world, so I didn't immediately plan to investigate. But I heard the noise again, and Ruth whispered that someone was at the door. So I slipped on my pants and moved toward the hall.

Our kitchen light had been left on, and I noticed smoke billowing out of the dishwasher. I hollered for the whole family to wake up. Robert was upstairs in a bedroom. Linda was in another. I saw Linda first and told her to call the fire department, but the telephone already was out of order.

"We better get out of here," I said. Smoke was everywhere.

Ruth had a big diamond I had bought her years earlier. She ran back for it and, when she did, she noticed that the back of the house was in flames. We didn't realize it then, but the upper floor we were on also had started to burn. We started to make our way out the front. We couldn't see, but there was a rail there to guide us down. When we reached the lower level, Linda could see flames up to the ceiling. I said we would have to duck down and cut to our left to make it outside. We made it.

A minute after we had safely left the living room, it was in flames.

Ruth's car was parked in front of mine. I had a company car, and I felt in my pants pocket for the keys. I had them, but all the electrical wires already had dropped close to the car. I figured I had read too many stories about people being electrocuted, so I just stood there and watched it burn. Fire already had consumed Ruth's car. The fire burned the tires off our Jeep, parked in an empty lot next door. We lost everything we had at our home there. Robert played the Trombone at the time — he was an all-state performer in high school in the early 70s. The horn simply melted away, and the fire burned every bit of the company car down to the axle.

The day before, Ruth had called in some servicemen to look at the dryer, which had been overheating. We think the fire may have started in the downstairs laundry room. It must have gotten so hot from the fire there that the pipes in the shower vibrated against each other, causing the noise that woke us.

That's some of the "good luck" and "good Lord" I was talking about earlier.

We never built back at the beach. Ruth and I grew apart. After 31 years of marriage, she and I divorced in 1978. I never expected my accidental meeting with Anne Blizzard at the Charlotte/Douglas International Airport one day to become an event that would so drastically change my personal life for the better. But there she was, and not many months later, I was proposing marriage to her in a crowded Athens restaurant.

Anne was 32 then and a successful dress designer. She says she was totally satisfied with her career and not even thinking about marriage — to anyone. I saved my best selling job ever for the courtship of her. We married in a small evening service at First Presbyterian Church in Salisbury on March 22, 1980, and our years together have been the happiest of my life.

Anne had confidence that her family and I would hit it off. Her father, Col. Joe Blizzard, had been a career military man and just the kind of authority figure I had butted heads with during my stint in the Army. I had some concerns about our first meeting, when Anne was "presenting" me to the family.

"Ralph," she said, "you don't have to worry. We'll have dinner about 6:30. Daddy goes to bed about 8 o'clock, so you don't have to worry about this first meeting and how it's going to go."

At the time, Joe Blizzard had retired from the military and was serving as a golf pro at the Myrtle Beach Air Force Base. Anne assured me that he awoke at 4 a.m. each day to make sure every blade of grass on his course was standing at attention. He usually went to bed early. Well, I must have made a good first impression because we were still going strong at 11:30 that first night. Anne's parents have become great friends. Joe has taught me how to play golf. And Anne and I have included them in many of our trips. It's the best present I could give Anne, who loves being with her folks as much as possible.

After I became 65 in 1985, I turned over responsibility for the company's day-to-day operations to Tom Smith. I spent less time at the office and more time traveling. Anne quickly learned how dangerous it is to leave me alone with a travel brochure. She likes to say we've been around the world, twice. We spent our first anniversary at the Taj Mahal. We've been to Kenya and Bangkok twice and several times to Egypt, New Zealand and Australia.

One of our most enjoyable trips was made with my former wife's sister Ruby and her husband Raymond Boggs. Anne and I took them on a trip to Africa to help settle an old debt. It was around 1954 after I had sold the new Oldsmobile I had bought after the war. I was driving an old Nash that used 10 quarts of oil on a trip to Southport and back. Raymond is a jack-of-all-trades and he heard about my car trouble. He said that if I would buy a set of rings, he would put them in for me. That solved the problem and I promised him that if I ever got any money, we would go on a trip. It took 40 years to fulfill that promise, but I am certain they feel adequately repaid for the repair job.

I bet we've taken 85 to 100 people as our guests to Las Vegas to see the shows. Sometimes I gamble. I have a unique system for playing blackjack. Nobody else in the United States uses it, to my knowledge, and I have not lost in 12 years. All you do is bet $5. If you lose, you double the bet, and you keep doubling it until you win. When you reach the table's limit, which is $5,000, you would have to have lost 11 times straight to be making that kind of bet. Jimmy the Greek says the dealer goes busted 30 percent of the time. Having that background knowledge, I devised this system.

If the table didn't have a limit, there's no way on earth I'd ever lose. I could go $20,000, $40,000, or $80,000, but sooner or later, I'd be bound to win. So if the tables had no limit, no one could lose — if he had enough money to bet in the first place.

I've had people say, "Oh, I've tried your system and it didn't work."

"You lost 11 times in a row?" I ask.

"Heck, no."

"Well, then, you didn't try my system. You quit somewhere along the line."

No, I haven't lost in 12 years. One day they'll hook me, but I'm so far ahead now it won't matter. I don't really enjoy playing that much because there's no decision-making the way I play. I just sit there. If I have 12 or more, I always stand pat. The secret to my system is to never go busted. I might hit a blackjack, or I might have 20 and the dealer has 19. It's the nearest thing to foolproof that can be.

We also take plenty of trips to Sarasota, Florida, where we have a modest home, but we could never live there full-time because Florida has an intangibles tax that's higher than North Carolina's. Anne enjoys the Florida home a lot.

I often speak to civic groups when I visit Florida. I welcome that opportunity because I give each person in the audience a two-dollar gift certificate to Food Lion. Competition among grocery stores is tougher in Florida, than many other Food Lion haunts, so I make a pitch for the company whenever I can.

Back at my Catawba College office in Salisbury, I answer a lot of calls and respond in writing to friends and people seeking money or advice I tell Anne that I shouldn't be identified with LFPINC any longer. The new initials are LPCINC — for Lowest-Priced Consultant in North Carolina. I charge nothing.

Several years ago, I received a call from the staff of "Lifestyles of the Rich and Famous." Robin Leach wanted me for the subject of one of his shows. I explained that their theme was "Caviar Wishes and Champagne Desires" whereas mine was Coca-Cola and hamburgers. I told them I was definitely not the type person for "Lifestyles of the Rich and Famous" and refused to be on the program.

The show's crew came to Salisbury anyway and interviewed stockholders and visited Catawba College, Nazareth Children's Home and other points. The show was broadcast, but I didn't even stay up to watch it.

When I walked into College Barbecue the next morning for my usual breakfast, several people said they had seen me on television.

"No way," I said.

One wanted to bet me $100 that I had been on "Lifestyles of the Rich and Famous."

If he had said $5, I would have taken the bet. But nobody bets $100 unless they know something.

Robin Leach's crew had gotten a tape of an interview I had done in Columbia, South Carolina, and used portions of it to make it appear that I was being interviewed by "Lifestyles of the Rich and Famous."

I called the show's producers and told them that under normal conditions I would have objected strenuously to their use of the tape without my permission, but since they made me look so good I had no complaints.

It wasn't until later that I realized that being on the show had its drawbacks. I began to receive requests from all over the United States from people asking me to fund projects or pay for medical expenses or trips and what have you. The show is repeated occasionally, and I can always tell because of the mail that pours in asking for money.

I've gotten a lot of good publicity for the success of Food Lion. I always try to give credit to the thousands of people who work so hard to put Food Lion's customers first and make the company grow.

I was invited by the Entrepreneur Association of America to be a speaker at its state convention in Raleigh. I was a member of a panel and was introduced by North Carolina Lieutenant Governor Jim Gardner. He mentioned the thousands of people who had put LFPINC bumper stickers on their cars and how difficult it was for a politician to get that kind of support.

"Jim," I said when it was my turn to speak, "if you had saved North Carolina taxpayers six to eight percent on their tax bills as I have saved them on their groceries, I feel certain they would be inclined to put your stickers on their cars."

Sitting at the head table, I had the opportunity to meet Wilson Harrell, publisher of *INC* magazine, sponsor of the Entrepreneur of the Year program along with Merrill Lynch and Ernst & Young. The panel discussion was well received, and I returned to Salisbury. The next day I got a telephone call from Dan Gardner of Merrill Lynch, asking me to fill in as a speaker for a luncheon the next day. I told him that he had heard the only speech I knew, and I didn't think the group should have to listen to it twice. He explained that I had spoken to North Carolina winners, but this luncheon was for 800 national winners. Ted Turner of Turner Broadcasting was to be the speaker but had to cancel because of illness.

After the speech, the organizers called my secretary, Kathy Martin, wanting to send a $2,000 honorarium. She told them she felt certain I would want it to go to Nazareth Children's Home. I told Kathy later that anytime anyone was willing to pay me $2,000 to let me made the decision as to whether I needed the money worse than my charity. Of course, I was kidding.

It was those two speeches about the success of Food Lion that led me to receive the Lifetime Achievement Award as the 1990 National Entrepreneur of the Year sponsored by Merrill Lynch, Inc., and Ernst & Young.

I'm a firm believer in getting back to people. If a person goes to the trouble of writing me, I owe him a reply. It burns me up when someone doesn't reply to a letter I've written. I'll take a copy of my original letter and write on the bottom, "This is the letter I wrote to you the last time. How about writing on it, 'Go to hell' and sending it back. At least I'll know you got the letter."

The purpose of a letter is to communicate. If you have to stir somebody up and make him mad, well, that's what you should do.

I dash off letters to politicians a lot, just to offer some of my ideas or to point out ways government could operate more efficiently. It's frustrating. I wrote Sen. Strom Thurmond once about my affordable housing project. I received a letter back from his office about the defense budget. I hadn't asked him a thing about the defense budget. Someone in his office pressed the wrong button for the wrong form letter.

Don't misunderstand. I believe in form letters. Food Lion has a standard lease, for example. When it's opening 100 stores a year, it makes little sense to have 100 different lease forms. And don't use the other guy's leases. Make him use yours and make it fair. You're saving him money. When I was at Food Lion and opening new stores, it took only about five minutes to read a lease.

I'm a firm believer in doing things the smart way. That's why Ross Perot's candidacy intrigued me in 1992. Nobody in government ever talks about cutting expenses. I'm for someone such as Perot who would go up there and look at every item and tell the people how out of control things are.

I've been asked plenty of times to run for political office, and I've come close on occasion. A couple of times, I'd wake up at 5 in the morning and think, "Gosh, I should run for something. I might get elected." Then I realized, hey, I could be elected. The thought brings me to my senses. But if I were a candidate, I'd run for Senate or Congress, but only if a guy like Perot were president. Right now, you've got to go along to get along, and that would drive me up the wall.

I decided long ago that if I ever run for office, my campaign theme would be: "Vote for me this time because you won't the next time." If I were elected, I would do what I think is right, and that wouldn't be very popular. Lobbyists, special interest groups and 50 telephone calls wouldn't have any influence with me.

It reminds me of the little boy who wrote to a company and asked, "Can you use a million frog skins?" An official of the company wrote back and said, "Son, yes, we'd be delighted. Ship them." In about two weeks, he received a box with four frog skins in it. The boy included a note, "Dear sir, *the noise fooled me.*"

And that's what happens. Congressmen go to Washington and because they receive a hundred telephone calls out of six million citizens, they wrongly believe they're hearing a consensus of opinion. It often is just a special interest group looking after its own members.

Of course, when I was running Food Lion, I never expressed a political opinion, because I don't believe the management of a publicly held company has the right to select a candidate and publicly support him. A landslide in politics is a 55 to 45 percent win. In the grocery business, you cater to everybody. Why alienate 45 percent of your customers? Or 55 percent?

Anybody likes to express his or her political opinion. If you own 100 percent of the company, go ahead. But if you have 17,000 shareholders — or even two shareholders — you've got an obligation to them not to do anything detrimental to business.

Who knows, politics could still be in the future. I'm only 73.

On the matter of age, Anne says she has never heard me say, "I'm tired." No matter how many hours of sleep I get, I wake up feeling good and I attack the day at full speed. Anne also says I have only one mood — happy. Well, worrying never accomplished much. I recall Tom Smith calling me about 3 o'clock one morning to inform me that our Monroe, North Carolina, store was burning down.

"We've got insurance on it," I assured him.

"I've sent the refrigerated truck over to haul the frozen food away," Tom said.

"Don't do that," I replied, happy that I could still think this quickly at 3 a.m. "You're going to mess up the inventory. It's insured. If we start moving stuff out, there's going to be an argument over how much we moved out. You get hold of that truck and stop it. And go ahead and go back to sleep. The fire department is down there."

I went back to sleep without a problem. I simply do the best I can during the day. Once my head hits the pillow, I'm usually asleep within a minute. Anne is just the opposite. She's thinking about 80 different things and has a miserable time falling asleep.

Anne receives a lot of credit for loosening me up. She jokes that when we first were married I wore a necktie to bed with my pajamas. She definitely has helped with my wardrobe. About 20 years ago, I lost a lot of my ability to taste certain things. I'm also color blind — that and having no "taste" must have combined for the look I received one day when I returned home from the office.

"Did you wear that to work," Anne asked.

"What's wrong with it?" I answered.

I had on navy pants, a black and white coat and a different-colored navy tie. Pretty dark, I was told. Anne usually lays out my clothes, except for that morning. When she goes on a trip or to see her parents alone, she puts out each day's clothes with a note attached to the individual sets. A note might say, "Wear this for golf Wednesday and have a great game."

One day the girls at the office knew Anne was out of town. They found this note on me that said, "It's Tuesday. Have a wonderful day at work. I'll see you when I get home."

With the years, I've lost some hearing. I need hearing aids for both ears. Each ear has a different problem: One requires amplification; the other, clarification. I distressed Anne for a time by not wearing both of them. I complained that I couldn't concentrate by wearing both at one time. I needed that quiet, but I've since given in to her argument that each aid serves a different purpose and normally I wear at least one.

Several days ago, I was having my usual breakfast at College Barbecue sitting alone in a booth. Wes Miller, a friend, came over and said "I like the Plaza."

I replied, "Great, I am glad."

Wes moved to the counter for service, and I really had no idea what Wes had said to me. I put my hearing aids in and went over to Wes and explained the situation.

He said, "I didn't think you understood me."

I asked, "Just what did you say?"

He replied, "I said your fly was open."

I looked down, and it was still open. With that, most everyone in the cafe burst out laughing.

Since this happened, I have been more conscious about wearing the hearing aids and especially about zipping up my fly!

I'm not too mechanically inclined. I'm still one of the best at arithmetic, but when it comes to something such as hanging a picture, Anne can have it nailed to the wall while I'm complaining that we haven't figured out where the nail should go.

"I know where it goes," she'll say.

We have fun. She puts up with my habits, my need to be organized and my appreciation of surprises and practical jokes.

Once my poker-playing buddies were over at Ted Proctor's house on a night I was going to a party at Food Lion vice president Gene McKinley's home. About 11 p.m., as Anne and I were

driving home from Gene's, we realized we would be passing Ted's house. I said, "Let's stop, go in and see how the boys are doing." When we reached the door, I told Anne I was going to hide in the bushes.

"You go in and tell them you've been dropped off from the party, so you could get a ride home with Ralph."

I hid in the bushes, and Ted came to the door.

Anne said, "I've decided to ride home with Ralph."

She walked in to where the rest of the group was sitting around the poker table.

"Where is Ralph?" she asked.

"He's gone to my house to take a shower," Pete Robertson said.

"He's in the bathroom," another guy said.

Anne was laughing so hard by then but they think she's crying because I'm not there. After about three minutes, I walk in for a good laugh. I asked Gary Swartzbach what he had told Anne.

"I was just trying to think of a name of a good lawyer for you," he said.

Anne's father witnessed another of my practical jokes. This one involved an exploding golf ball I had in my possession on a golfing trip to Pinehurst, North Carolina. A broker friend of mine had invited Col. Blizzard and me for a weekend. With us were Ned Edwards of the Edwards brokerage firm and the national sales manager for White House products.

I kept wondering how I could use my exploding ball. My opportunity came at the first tee when the sales manager presented me with a sleeve of new golf balls. I knew then what I was going to do. I pretended that I was opening the sleeve when, in fact, I pulled the exploding ball out of my pocket and placed it on the tee.

I set up the scene beautifully, explaining how I had been taking lessons.

"Watch this swing," I boasted.

I hit the ball, and it just disintegrated. I immediately turned around and glared at the national sales manager.

"Is this your idea of a damn joke?" I demanded

I should mention that Food Lion was buying about $5 million a year from this guy named Jim.

"I'll kill the guy," Jim said. "I just bought these balls."

"No problem," I said. "But if this next ball explodes, I would start leaving if I were you."

I hit the next ball fine. I think Jim — he's about a three handicap — shot an eight on the first hole. By the third hole, I gave in and told him about my dirty trick.

As you may have figured out by now, my children did not follow in my footsteps at Food Lion. Linda worked briefly for the company in the 1970s and was instrumental in establishing our training program and effective scheduling for the workforce. But she wanted more excitement than Salisbury could offer. Now she's a successful management consultant in Charleston. I'm told she has a lot of my personality. Anne once described her as Ralph Ketner with breasts.

My son, Robert, has established himself as a Vice-President with Merrill Lynch in Greensboro, North Carolina. He has provided me with three grandchildren and a lot of fishing stories. Whenever Robert and I take a father-son fishing trip, some catastrophe happens.

Once, we were bringing our 14-foot Boston whaler back from a trip along the Atlantic Coast and our gas was running low. So we hugged the shore as much as we could. We should have worried more about choppy water. A wave hit us broadside and turned the boat over. It turned out we were in four feet of water, but we lost a lot of our fishing gear with the spill.

On a later fishing expedition on a Rowan County lake, we were coming back to dock after a fairly successful day. I picked up the anchor to heave it onto the dock but missed and went into the water head first. Just one more drenching and one more humbling experience.

The worst was yet to come. Robert and I were guests of Jeno Pelucci, a major food dealer, in Canada. Jeno had another engagement and couldn't be on the water with us. I was in a boat with Jeno's national sales manager. Robert was in another boat nearby. Before we left, Jeno had warned us of some turbulent rapids at one end of the lake. Don't let your motor die near the rapids, Jeno warned, or you may be swept into them.

That's what happened to the sales manager and me. He had hooked a big fish and was trying to bring him in when our motor died near the rapids. We were swept over the rapids but survived without injury. The boat had a little damage and, again, we lost some gear.

When we finally got up with Robert again, I asked the other guy in his boat what my son was doing as I disappeared over the rapids.

"I don't know exactly," he said. "But I did see him pull out his briefcase and start reading what looked like a will."

It seems like only yesterday sometimes that my own grocer father died without a will and set into motion a miraculous chain of events. I marvel sometimes at how a stubborn, shy and independent kid like me ever reached this point and can look back on such a wonderful life, filled with great friends and family. And it's by no means over.

I goof off a lot now, and I don't like it. Ideas keep flooding into my head — so much so that Anne says she'll never have to worry about another woman. Lately, I've been toying with the idea of low-price prescription medicines and returning to that concept on a real basis — two to three stores at first. I don't want to make any profit, so it's hard to find a business partner or investors. I don't really need investors, I guess, but I would if I ever take the concept nationwide.

Oops, here I go again. Thinking big.

Editorial

Painful parting

■ *Ralph Ketner-Food Lion split makes the unthinkable a reality*

❝It's sort of like a divorce," Ralph Ketner said this week about his stunning departure from Food Lion, the grocery company he helped found and inspire.

Ketner's comparison is apt. By deciding not to seek re-election to Food Lion's

Ketner

board of directors, Ketner has severed a relationship that seemed unshakeable.

Food Lion without Ralph Ketner? Impossible!

Yet it's true. And at a time when Salisbury's grocery chain is still working to overcome the fallout from the "PrimeTime Live" program and the never-ending taunting from union supporters, Ketner's departure is doubly painful.

Because Ketner's disagreements with Food Lion were so fundamental — he questioned the company's recent growth strategy and its response to the "PrimeTime Live" broadcast and congressional hearings — his decision to leave is understandable though still regrettable.

Uncommon marriage

Yet if a divorce is a time for sadness, it also provides a time to reflect on happier memories.

When Ketner, his brother Brown and Wilson Smith created Food Town (Food Lion's original incarnation) back in 1957, they did so largely with small investments from Rowan County friends and neighbors. Food Town provided an uncommon marriage of energy, ambition and creativity which eventually multiplied those meager investments into miraculous fortunes.

Ketner also well remembers the day in 1967 when he sequestered himself in a Charlotte motel room with five boxes of grocery invoices and an adding machine. Out of that marathon number-crunching session emerged the pricing concept that has lifted Food Lion to towering heights: Lowest Food Prices in North Carolina, soon known by its ubiquitous bumpersticker abbreviation, LFPINC.

Labeled fittingly at the time as "The Big Change," Ketner's concept of "everyday low prices," an elegantly devised series of across-the-board price cuts, changed the grocery industry forever.

Changes

As he steps down from the Food Lion board, Ketner clearly wishes the company well. And as Food Lion Vice President Vince Watkins noted, Ketner will now have more time to devote to the many charitable endeavors he and his wife, Anne, have supported.

Ketner's successor as a Food Lion director, Dr. Bernard Franklin, president of Livingstone College, will clearly bring a new perspective as the first African American on the board. A man of unquestioned integrity, Franklin has repeatedly demonstrated his management capabilities and vision at Livingstone, which has seen enormous improvements in recent years. His input on the Food Lion board should be welcomed and respected.

Still, there's no denying that Ralph Ketner's departure from Food Lion marked one of the saddest points in Rowan County history. Everyone in Rowan County is a child of this divorce.

Epilogue

When I come up against a brick wall, I don't bang my head against it. That just gives me a headache, and I've reached the point in life where I've had all the headaches I want.

So with a lot of sadness, I decided to leave the board of Food Lion in April 1993. It was sort of like a divorce where two people had grown apart over the years.

My disagreements with President Tom Smith and others were so fundamental that it seemed pointless to remain. Food Lion's decision to expand into Texas, its response to ABC's "Prime-Time Live" show and the handling of the Congressional hearing before U. S. Rep. Lantos on behalf of the Labor Department were three of many areas where we were at odds.

Texas: Before moving into Texas, our policy had always been to open new stores in states joining present operations. This practice guarantees customer awareness and knowledge of Food Lion due to overlapping of television, newspaper, radio and word-of-mouth exposure. In moving to Texas, we jumped several states and, as a result, our potential customer base knew absolutely nothing about Food Lion.

This problem alone was tremendous, but because of this "jump" it was necessary that a warehouse be opened almost simultaneously with 40 to 50 stores. To accomplish this, it was necessary to again change a Food Lion Policy. In the past, we had always leased our stores, but in order to guarantee 40 to 50 openings at once, it was necessary to buy property and to build our own stores. This required much more cash and a much greater gamble. Another problem was that getting 40 to 50 stores opened in approximately twelve months meant accepting questionable locations.

I cannot help but think that Food Lion's purchase of a jet plane several years earlier played a part in the Texas decision. We had the plane — let's find a use for it.

"PrimeTime Live:" For months, Food Lion management was aware that they would be the focus of an unflattering TV segment. Even though I was a director, I first became aware of the forthcoming program when I read of it in the newspaper. To this day, I don't know exactly what was known by Tom Smith and others at headquarters. I found out much later that a decision was made — not by the board of directors — to hire a public relations firm. This, in my opinion was a tremendous mistake, as it seemed that they continued to keep the issue before the public rather than working to keep it out of the news.

I heard from someone — not as a director and not from Tom Smith — that most Food Lion executives planned to watch "PrimeTime Live" on a large screen television at Food Lion headquarters. I went out, uninvited, to watch it with them. I didn't see Tom Smith. He was upstairs working with the public relations people to prepare his rebuttal to the program. Keep in mind this was only minutes away from the airing of the program. For approximately three months, it was known that the program was coming, yet only minutes before, Tom was rehearsing. During those three months, we could, and should, have prepared two or three scenarios — the first to be used if the program only made Food Lion look **BAD**; the second if the program made Food Lion look **VERY BAD**, and the third to be used if the program made Food Lion look **TERRIBLE**, which it did. Instead, the public relations firm had Tom go on television live immediately after the program. Tom was agitated, and it clearly showed.

It was obvious to everyone that the show was going to create a tremendous problem for Food Lion, and would drastically hurt our sales and profits. It was equally obvious that many lies were told, and many products not carried by Food Lion were used as having been a part of "PrimeTime Live's" "staging." Diane Sawyer admitted the following week on "PrimeTime Live" that some of the items used were in error and were items not carried by Food Lion.

The morning after the show, I awoke around 5 a.m. and started asking myself what might be done to counteract the show. I came up with what I thought was a great idea:

> "I, personally, as a co-founder and director of the company would immediately call a press conference in Washington, D.C., inviting all news media. I would refer to the "PrimeTime Live" program, identify myself as co-founder in 1957 and as a director for 35 years, president for 23 years, and chairman of the board for 33 years. I would then unfold a giant check in the amount of $1 million, payable to Diane Sawyer, or charity of her choice. I would explain to the media that this was my personal offer and not funds of Food Lion. This check was to be hers if all the people on her program would take — and pass — a lie detector test. I would demand that she publicize my offer on her next "PrimeTime Live" program. I felt certain that NBC and CBS would do so as would other media."

I called Tom Smith early that morning and told him what I wanted to do. His first reaction was that this would be great. Later, he called to tell me they (I don't know to this day the identity of *they*) decided not to accept my offer, as they felt it would keep the matter stirred up. I feel that if my offer had been ac-

217

cepted, and the public relations firm fired, the issue would have been short-lived, especially in view of the fact that during my discussion with Tom I increased my offer to Diane Sawyer to $5 million.

I then suggested that consideration be given to a $1 million lottery on a monthly basis. The cost of this would not have been much over $600,000, as lotteries are normally paid out over a 20-year period, thus reducing the cost to somewhere in the neighborhood of 60 percent of the dollar prize.

To offer the $1 million lottery on a monthly basis would have cost one-tenth of one percent of sales. Everyone at the company was excited about this promotion, and Joe Hall, the head buyer, had negotiated with a firm specializing in lotteries to have the tickets printed and made other arrangements. In a telephone conversation with members of the board in Brussels, Gui de Vaucleroy said that we should not consider this promotion as no one would be interested in any type lottery with only one winner. I then said, "Gui, last week I was in Florida where more than 8 million people paid $1 each to purchase lottery tickets with basically one winner. I believe you are completely mistaken." Gui made the decision to kill the promotion. It was necessary that the meeting be put on hold for a few minutes while Tom sent information to Joe Hall to notify the people printing the tickets that the promotion was dead.

Congressional hearing: I feel that Tom Smith should have gone to Washington himself to address the Congressional hearing. Instead, he sent a vice president. I know that if I had still been running the company, no one could have prevented me as president and chairman from going to represent Food Lion.

Other factors, all discussed with Tom Smith or members of the board, that entered my decision not to stand for re-election are listed on the following pages.

1. For years, I felt that Tom was spending considerable time making television commercials and public appearances promoting Tom Smith rather than Food Lion.

2. I felt that activity on behalf of a political party was not in the best interest of Food Lion. I repeated this many, many times over the years while I was running the company, stating that under no conditions should a publicly held company become involved with political candidates. Since my departure, I've often read of political events sponsored by Food Lion executives. Another departure from the philosophy and formula which brought our success.

3. Regarding Food Lion's profit-sharing payments for 1992, I felt that the decision to pay 15 percent of eligible employees' earnings rather than 20 percent of pre-tax earnings was wrong. As a result, Food Lion paid approximately $82 million whereas 20% of pre-tax earnings would have amounted to approximately $58 million, a difference of $24 million. In 1963 when we set up our Profit Sharing Plan, the decision was made to pay either 15% of eligible employees earnings or 20% of pre-tax earnings — **whichever was lower.** In 1984 the Board changed the formula to read that the Board would decide the amount to be distributed to Profit Sharing but that same could not exceed the legal maximum of 15% of eligible employees earnings. This action was taken to remove the "floor" in the event the Board should at some point feel it not in the best interest of the company to pay 20% of pre-tax earnings.

If the Board decides again this year to pay 15% of eligible employees earnings rather than 20% of pre-tax earnings, it will cost Food Lion shareholders not $24 million as it did in 1992, but approximately $45 million. This is because of less earnings and more eligible employees. I hope the Board does not repeat this "mistake." Only time will tell.

I know that several people at the May 1993 shareholders meeting submitted questions in writing asking Tom about this excess payment of $24 million, but either he did not receive the question (!), or chose not to answer it. When Tom first said he had answered all question cards, there were approximately 60 people who raised their hands to signal their questions had not been answered.

4. On many occasions, I discussed with Tom the fact that I felt Vince Watkins was doing an extremely poor job in his news releases regarding happenings at Food Lion. Vince resigned from Food Lion in 1993.

5. I felt that the program "Save the Lion" was poorly conceived, as it indicated that the lion was dying, and this certainly was not the message that we wanted our customers to hear.

6. I was often embarrassed as a board member to be unaware of situations that were happening until reading about them in the newspaper. The newspaper was the first notice I had regarding the Congressional hearing where John Watkins appeared. Earnings reports came to me by way of the newspaper, as did the story about "Prime-Time Live." The decision to delay the dividend due February 1, 1993, was unknown to me until a shareholder called asking when he might expect to receive same.

7. The hiring of the public relations firm was not made known to the board of directors, or at least not to this member of the board until I read of same in the newspaper.

8. I am quoting the closing paragraph of a letter to Tom Smith from Vince Watkins and Bill McCanless, Food Lion's attorney. The letter is dated November 16, 1992, eleven days **after** the "PrimeTime Live" program:

"Update on PTL"

"Looking at the graphs of the press and the comeback of our store sales, we have succeeded to date. This has been a traditional crisis management case where it is a national story for less than a week. With our assistance, the press coverage has died. Now our strategy is to bring the few customers who have not come back into our stores through traditional Food Lion marketing methods, increasing advertising and promotions. We are right on target. Coverage has decreased substantially. And, numbers don't lie."

This is the kind of information upon which Tom was relying.

9. During 1992 and the first two months of 1993, we paid public relations firms over $1.7 million and spent over $370,000 to distribute 60,000 videos rebutting the "PrimeTime Live" show. These 60,000 videos were sent to Food Lion's 60,000 employees. The quality was poor, and, in my opinion, accomplished very little. During the six months between the "PrimeTime Live" show and the annual meeting, Tom Smith stated he had no time to write even the first letter to the shareholders explaining to them the problems encountered. This, to me, was inexcusable.

10. I mailed this letter to Tom Smith on March 15, 1993. I never received a reply from Tom even though I made several follow-ups.

Mr. Tom E. Smith
President & Chairman of the Board
Food Lion, Inc.
P. O. Box 1330
Salisbury, NC 28144

Dear Tom:

I feel that for the first time you will face hostile shareholders at Food Lion's annual meeting this year. During the years Brown attempted to take over Food Town, I was confronted with hostile shareholders at every meeting.

I found it extremely necessary to plan for these hostile meetings by playing "the devil's advocate" by asking myself what would be the worse possible questions to be asked. I suggest you prepare accordingly.

I am listing below some questions I feel might be raised and, as a director, I would like answers to same from you or your office.

1. Why was approximately $24,000,000 extra paid into Profit Sharing for the year 1992? Twenty percent pre-tax earnings would have been approximately $58,000,000, yet $82,000,000 was paid.

2. What was the total cost for our privately owned airplane for 1992?

   A. How many trips were made by you to visit stores and warehouses?
   B. How many trips to pick up or return Delhaize members?
   C. How many other trips?
   D. Average cost per trip?

3. What was total $ amount paid to Public Relations firm in 1992? $ _____

   January '93?_____   February '93?_____

222

4. This I am certain will not come up, but what did we pay as dues to FMI last year? Do you recommend continuing? If so, why?

5. Why you and Vince sponsored political rallies?

6. Why John Watkins was spokesman at Congressional hearings?

7. Why Vince and others are quoted more often than you?

8. Why with two months notice was Food Lion unprepared for a *PrimeTime Live* rebuttal?

9. Why Food Lion has a PAC?

10. Does Food Lion pay anything to sponsor NASCAR team?

11. Justification for securing $1,800,000 for Tom Smith's scholarships at Catawba?

12. Why the decision was made to change the concept of an "ever-increasing circle" and jump to Texas?

13. Why the decision was made to own rather than lease stores?

14. Justification for printing, distributing, etc. 60,000 videos on *PrimeTime Live* but having no time for informing shareholders. Question: What was *total cost* for these 60,000 tapes?

15. Why has so little been done to explain to the public what constitutes "child labor violations?"

16. Why was there no follow-through on the offer by Colonel Fred Oettinger's of Clarksville, Virginia, to bring, at his expense, to Salisbury a petition with 3,000 signatures urging you to bring a Food Lion to Clarksville? Certainly a good publicity opportunity.

    I understand two or more Food Lion people promised to "get back to him," but none did.

17. I understand we quit using Salisbury-Rowan Merchants Association for reference checks on employee applicants and gave this business to a firm in Florida, thus causing ill will from the members of the local association.

18. Why stockholders were not told they would not receive their dividends on February 1, as this was the custom for the last ten years or so?

Tom, I realize that in the past years you have never once asked for my advice or my ideas on any subject, and, no doubt, you will feel this letter is uncalled for—and perhaps it is. I hope that you are prepared to answer the above questions and the many other questions that might be raised.

As a director, I would appreciate answers to questions 2, 3, 4, 10, 14, 16, and 17.

Tom, I hope that I am wrong about the upcoming annual meeting, but I feel it might be worse than either of us anticipates.

Regards,
Ralph W. Ketner

11. A number of people questioned the cash bonus paid Tom Smith and other key employees for 1992. I was not one of these, as I knew the formula upon which bonuses were paid to them. The formula required first a 15% return **after taxes** on beginning equity for the year and, once this requirement was met, certain employees shared a percentage of the excess. In 1992, these requirements were met; **however,** I do not believe there is any possibility of after-tax earnings for 1993 equaling 15% of beginning equity, therefore, I do not feel that Tom and the other executives **will earn, or receive,** cash bonuses for 1993. Here, too, only time will tell.

These are just a few of the points which resulted in my decision not to stand for re-election as a director in May 1993. I still own a considerable number of shares of Food Lion stock and sincerely hope and pray that the worst is behind and that management can, and will, move forward.

I have thought for some time as to how to close this book. I am indebted to so many people that it would be impossible to list them all, so I will not try.

I do realize, however, that my greatest debt is to my Lord and, therefore, have decided to close with my very favorite poem.

Heaven's Grocery Store

While walking down Life's Highway some time ago,
I saw a sign that read "Heaven's Grocery Store."
As I got a little closer, the door came open wide,
and then I suddenly realized I was drawn right inside.

I saw a host of angels; they were standing everywhere,
one handed me a basket and said, "My child, shop with care."
Everything a Christian needed was in that Grocery Store,
and what you couldn't carry, you could come back tomorrow for.

First I got some PATIENCE, LOVE was in the same row,
further down was UNDERSTANDING, needed wherever you go.
I picked up a box of COURAGE to help me run this race,
my basket was getting full when I remembered I needed GRACE.

I didn't forget SALVATION, for SALVATION that was free,
so I tried to get enough of that to save both you and me.
Then I started up to the counter to pay my grocery bill,
for I thought I had everything to do the Master's Will.

As I went up the aisle I saw PRAYER, and I threw some in,
for I knew when I stepped outside, I would run right into sin.
PEACE and JOY were plentiful, they were on the top shelf,
SONG and PRAISES were hanging near, so I just helped myself.

And then to the Angel at the door I asked, "How much do I owe?"
He smiled and said, "Just take them everywhere you go."
I smiled at him and said, "Now really, how much do I owe?"
*"My child," he said, "**Christ paid your bill a long time ago.**"*

Anonymous

Thank you for taking the time to read my story.

I hope you've gotten a sense of the fun I've had with a myraid of challenges and opportunities.

Ralph W. Ketner

Lightning Source UK Ltd.
Milton Keynes UK
UKHW010957030323
417983UK00006B/359

9 780367 756727